Reaching
for a Star

The Extraordinary Life of MILAN KROUPA

REACHING
FOR A STAR

JOSEF ČERMÁK
Translated by Paul Wilson

Figure 1
Vancouver / Berkeley

Copyright © 2016 by Josef Čermák
Translation copyright © 2016 by Paul Wilson
Translated from the original Czech (*Rozlet: příběhy Milana Kroupy*) published in 2014

16 17 18 19 20 5 4 3 2 1

Cataloguing data available from Library and Archives Canada
ISBN 978-1-927958-59-9 (hbk.)
ISBN 978-1-927958-75-9 (ebook)
ISBN 978-1-927958-77-3 (pdf)

Editing by Shirarose Wilensky
Design by Natalie Olsen
Front jacket photograph by Nicolas Balcazar
Printed and bound in Canada by Friesens
Distributed in the U.S. by Publishers Group West

Figure 1 Publishing Inc.
Vancouver BC Canada
www.figure1pub.com

Millions of stars are

constantly flying towards us...

millions of opportunities...

LADISLAV KROUPA, SR.

CONTENTS

Two Episodes

TWO **EPISODES** play an unusually significant role in Milan Kroupa's professional life: the first marked the beginning of his soccer career as a child in his native Czechoslovakia; the second took place after he had become a successful Canadian entrepreneur, while flying several hundred metres above the fertile countryside a few kilometres west of the prosperous Ontario city of Barrie, an hour's drive north of Toronto.

Milan Kroupa is a creative soul who does not insist that life's events follow a logical order, so let us start with the second episode, in an ultra-light aircraft west of Barrie.

It was April 2003. Milan was practising stalls with his flying instructor. At the same time, he was observing the countryside below, which reminded him of the landscape around the legendary Czech mountain Říp, close to his native Slánsko in Bohemia, north of Prague, and of the farmland along the Labe River, which at the end of July was always bright with golden fields of ripening wheat. There was perhaps only one difference: the countryside below him had just recently shed its covering of snow and would soon begin to display the first slender shoots of winter wheat. He noticed the telltale signs of something else, something that looked very much like a dilapidated runway overgrown with brush and weeds. His instructor explained to him that it was an old aerodrome from the Second World War that had been closed down and all its buildings dismantled. Later, he learned this area was called Edenvale, literally "paradise valley."

Most people would have done little more with this information than take note, but Milan Kroupa is different. You could probably say that his nose for business is not unlike that of Jaroslav Mraz, the famous owner of a light airplane factory in the former Czechoslovakia, of whom his employees used to say: "If the old man learned there'd be an epidemic of diarrhea tomorrow, he'd have started making bedpans yesterday."

Kroupa is not a man of many words, but his mind is always alert. He's not a theoretician, even though he thinks a lot about things such as truth and justice, and what an individual can contribute to the world. His brain might well have been the creation of some entrepreneurial mastermind who worried, with half the world dominated by Communism, that brilliant entrepreneurs were in danger of going extinct. Kroupa's head always seems to be teeming with practical problems that demand practical solutions. And instead of making up excuses for doing nothing, he solves them.

In 2003, after seeing the crumbling and weed-infested runway, he bought the airport. Later in this story, we will learn how that came about and what he turned it into.

But first, let us return to Kroupa's childhood.

WHAT A FROZEN RIVER or pond or an artificial ice rink is to Canadian kids in winter, a grassy village square or a meadow is to European kids, and certainly to Czech children. At each end of the playing area, Czech boys would improvise goalposts out of shirts or schoolbags, and between these two goals a battle for the ball played out, even though in those days the ball was often just a tight bundle of rags. By the time Milan began to take an interest in soccer, the boys were still playing in a meadow, but they were using a real soccer ball. They flaunted their skills the way boys do, by adopting the names of famous stars from the best-known Prague sports clubs, such as Sparta and Slavia.

Milan's brother, Ladislav (Lad'a for short); his mother, Maria; and Milan, 1952.

3

For a long time — and this used to bother Milan a lot — he couldn't find a position in which he was outstanding. He was especially annoyed that he wasn't chosen to play in a match between his native village, Dřetovice, and the neighbouring village of Stehelčeves. Each community was small, comprising no more than about three hundred households, but the atmosphere at the game was as tense as at any match between two continents. The rivalry was intense. It was a great honour to be chosen to play; to be rejected was the ultimate dishonour. Milan was never one to accept defeat or rejection easily, and when he didn't see his name on the roster, he assumed it was an oversight and approached the captain.

"So where am I going to play?" he said boldly.

The captain's reply stung Milan to the quick: "You're going to stand behind the left goalpost and watch."

The blow to his pride was not fatal, for Milan saw the captain's decision as proof of his inability to recognize genuine talent. He would show them!

Some weeks later, the boys were kicking a homemade ball around the newly constructed Dřetovice soccer pitch. Once again, there was no position for Milan. But he was already very perceptive and noticed there was no one in goal, so he stepped into the position. He felt somewhat reluctant, because he'd never played in goal before. But reluctant or not, he didn't hold back. The boys began peppering him with two balls at once. Perhaps they wanted to show him he didn't belong in goal — boys, after all, can be merciless — but to their surprise, and to his own as well, Milan managed to catch most of the balls or to deflect them. The admiration he saw in the boys' eyes ignited his ambition. Some of his moves were worthy of a circus acrobat. The father of one of his friends came up to Milan afterwards and said, "You've got talent, my lad! Work at it and you'll make something of yourself."

"Mummy, What Have You Done?"

MILAN WAS BORN on February 21, 1942, in a flour mill in Dřetovice, central Bohemia, close to two small cities, Kladno and Slaný. There were coal mines around Kladno, and the town was known for its steelworks and engineering industries. Slaný was known for its churches and its connection to Hussite history and the Reformation, in which fifteenth-century Catholics and Protestants took acrimonious turns wielding power in the town. It seems both antagonistic sides of the same religion forgot that the basis of their faith was a doctrine of self-effacing love.

Milan had hardly chosen the most auspicious date for his arrival on the planet. He was born into an inhospitable time in the middle of one of the most terrible conflicts in human history. It wasn't just that soldiers were dying at the front or that peaceful citizens were being

ABOVE LEFT

Milan with his father, 1943.

ABOVE RIGHT

The Kroupa family in the 1940s.

slaughtered in bombing raids, but millions of innocents were being transported to concentration camps and murdered in gas chambers. The grapes of wrath began to ripen when Winston Churchill greeted Neville Chamberlain — who returned from the Munich conference with an agreement that doomed Milan's homeland to Nazi occupation — with the words: "You had the choice between war and shame. You chose shame, and you will have war."

And they got it.

On September 3, 1939, Britain and France declared war on Germany, and Churchill took over as secretary of the navy, a position he held for eight months during one of the darkest periods in British history. The duel between a scion of a venerable English family and corporal Hitler had begun. Churchill wrote about the genesis of Hitler: "A great vacuum opened up and into it stepped a madman of terrible genius, expressing the most virulent hatred that had ever contaminated the human heart."

From that moment on, until December 11, 1941, when Germany and Italy declared war on the United States, Churchill carried the fate of the world on his shoulders. The stirring cadences of his oratory gave strength to the defeated, the discouraged, and the weary. On May 10, 1940, when he became prime minister, he said, "Gentlemen, we are alone. As for myself, I find it exciting." And then three days later, in his first speech to Parliament, he said, "I have nothing to offer but blood, toil, tears and sweat... You ask, what is our aim? I can answer in one word: It is victory, victory at all costs, victory in spite of all terror, victory, however long and hard the road may be; for without victory, there is no survival." (When he repeated the speech on the radio, he covered his mouth with his hands and added: "And we're going to beat them over the heads with beer bottles because that's about all we'll have.")

All of this happened before Milan was born, but the monstrous juggernaut of history continued after his birth. On April 27, 1942, when Milan was three months old, forty kilometres from Dřetovice, a group of six Czech parachutists, who had been trained in England, assassinated one of the most brutal Nazi leaders, the *Reichsprotektor* Reinhard Heydrich, as he was being driven to his office in Prague Castle. The commander-in-chief of the ss and the police at the office of the *Reichsprotektor* in Bohemia and Moravia, K.H. Frank, in a broadcast to the Czech nation, offered a reward of 10 million crowns for the arrest of the assassins. "Anyone who provides shelter or aid to the perpetrators, or who knows of their whereabouts, and fails to report this," he said, "will be shot, along with all of their family."

Heinrich Himmler, head of the ss, in a telegram to K.H. Frank on the same day, ordered the arrest of the entire Czech opposition intelligentsia and the execution of one hundred of its leading members.

On June 22, 1942, over dinner, Hitler said: "Wherever trains are derailed, or assassinations are carried out, or shelter is given to enemy parachutists, as in the case of Heydrich's assailants, the mayor of the community must be shot, the men deported or shot, and the women transferred to concentration camps."

The parachutists were eventually all caught and killed, but the Nazi fury came to within a mere six kilometres of the mill in which Milan was born. On June 24, 1942, the district commander of the state police in Prague, Doctor Geschenke, issued this statement:

On the Führer's orders a retaliatory measure was taken against the village of Lidice because the Czech parachutists, after exiting an English plane, stayed in this village and were supported by relatives of the Czech legion in England, as well as by citizens of this village. All of the 95 homes in the village were burnt to the ground, 199 male citizens 15 years old and over were shot on the spot, 184 women were taken to the concentration camp in Ravensbrück, seven women were sent to the police prison in Terezín, four pregnant women went to hospital in Prague, 88 children were sent to Łodze and seven one-year-olds were removed to a shelter in Prague. Three children will be taken to the territory of the old Reich for the purpose of Germanizing them.

Three-month-old Milan, however, had other worries. Shortly after his birth, he caught pneumonia, which probably had nothing to do with the fact that he was born at home, as was the custom at the time, rather than in a hospital, or that his mother was assisted not by an obstetrician, but rather by a midwife. He survived the first bout of pneumonia and, as though to demonstrate that even as a baby he could push the limits, he came down with a second bout three months after recovering from the first.

Because he was moody, disobedient, and willful, you might think he was a spoiled only child, but he wasn't. His mother had six children in all, but four were stillborn or died shortly after birth. Now he has only one brother, Ladislav (Lad'a), eight years his senior and his parents' second child.

The first childhood incident Milan clearly remembers took place in the kitchen when he was about three. He recalls having a pacifier in his mouth. The kitchen in the flour mill was large, because they cooked for the mill hands, who also took their meals there around a large table. That day, his mother was cooking lunch on the coal-fired stove, and she burned the food. Milan remembers precisely what happened next:

She turned on me and shouted, "And you can just keep quiet!" She snatched the pacifier out of my mouth and threw it in the stove. What I remember is how helpless I felt. I started crying and asked my mother, "Mummy, what have you done?" Mother later told me that my reaction was the greatest punishment she could have received. Even so, she didn't buy me a new pacifier. This was the beginning of my self-reliance and my independence.

Milan's Parents and Grandparents

MILAN'S MOTHER WAS CALLED MARIA; her maiden name was Dvořáková, and her mother was a Mansfeldová. Maria had three older brothers: Milan, Slavek, and Franta. She was what is sometimes called "an afterthought": she was ten years younger than her eldest brother. Her parents owned one of the largest farms in the village of Ruda U Nového Strašeci. The farm consisted of large fields, and Milan's grandparents raised many different domestic animals and also ran a pub. His grandfather was a well-regarded member of the community and served as mayor of the village for many years. Milan's mother told him how, when she was young, the family would ride to balls and other social events in a carriage pulled by a pair of proud horses, a very different kind of elegance than the kind provided by today's luxury automobiles. She recalled taking part in the

11

traditional celebrations at the end of harvest, and her stories evoked a world that was dismantled by two world conflicts and buried by galloping technology. Her parents died shortly before Milan was born, both from pneumonia.

Milan's maternal grandfather must have also been a bit like the founder of the Bata shoe company, Thomas Bat'a. Mr. Dvořák practised what today is called "responsible capitalism." He believed that entrepreneurs were responsible for the quality of life of their employees, and that all of us are, to a certain extent, responsible for each other.

One day, two boys appeared on the steps of the family pub; one was ten, the other twelve.

"They sat there all day," Milan says, "and in the evening, Grandpa asked them, 'Boys, aren't you going home?' In the end the boys confessed that their father had brought them there and told them that they should wait for him but that they knew he wasn't coming back. Their names were Vincent and Franta, and Grandpa took them under his wing and brought them up until they were adults."

Milan's maternal grandmother clearly shared her husband's philanthropic views. Although Milan's father, Ladislav, came from a working-class family, he was clever and entrepreneurial, but he could scarcely have been considered an ideal partner by Milan's mother's parents. Even so, Milan's maternal grandmother never tried to dissuade her daughter from marrying him, and she never tried to ease him out of the running by advancing the fortunes of other suitors. In fact, she went in the other direction. Just before the wedding, Milan's father, who had always wanted to have a business of his own and probably also wanted to show the parents of his future wife he came from good stock, leased a sawmill near Kladno. His future wife's

Milan's mother, Maria Dvořáková, 1930s.

Milan's father, Ladislav Kroupa, 1940s.

Růženka and František Dvořák. Milan's maternal grandparents.

mother declared she was not going to give her daughter away in marriage only to have her live in rental property, so she gave her future son-in-law 120,000 crowns. With this money, Milan's father bought not only the flour mill where Milan was born but also a sawmill in Srbeč, reassuring his future in-laws they need not fear for their daughter's future.

MILAN WORSHIPPED HIS FATHER, LADISLAV. To a considerable extent, his relationship with his father is reminiscent of the relationship between Thomas Bat'a Jr. and his father, who founded one of the largest private industrial enterprises in the world. Both men wanted to follow in their fathers' footsteps, and both wanted to remain faithful to their fathers' philosophies. Milan's paternal grandfather worked as a freelance carpenter; in other words, he worked on commission. His grandmother was a housewife.

"My father's mother, Granny Kroupová," Milan says, "was very tough on my mother. In moments of weakness, Mother would say she was 'mean.' She constantly criticized Mother, and Mother was never able to measure up, no matter what she did. She spent a lot of time crying but in the end pulled herself together and stood by her husband's side."

It can be said that the fates blessed Milan with good genes. It can also be said — as we will see — that Milan made the most of those genes.

"Sir, I'm a Thief!"

ALONG WITH THE FLOUR MILL in Dřetovice, where they spent the winter, Milan's family also owned a sawmill just outside Nové Strašecí, where Milan's father began manufacturing paintbrush handles from scrap wood he was reluctant to throw out. He found a market for them as far away as England.

They also owned a cottage just outside Srbeč, where they spent the summers. It was a wonderful place, Milan remembers, made of larch wood. It had a pond, where Milan and his brother and his cousin would go swimming. His father planted fruit trees, gooseberries, and straw-berries. "It was heaven on earth," Milan says. Milan spent the first six idyllic years of his childhood either at the family mill or at the cottage.

As a child, he was often alone, since his brother was eight years older than him. He didn't mind, because he could make good use of

his solitude, especially during the long winters in the flour mill. Being alone allowed him to cultivate his imagination. He often dreamed of having a farm, but he did more than dream; he actually built a model farm, complete with stables, in a sandbox. Then he took a corncob, stuck a nail in it, tied a string to the nail, and hitched it to a matchbox he filled with pebbles to represent pigs, and then drove them to "market." It was a well-organized and prosperous farm.

He would tell himself stories in which he already saw himself as a businessman. His daydreams were strongly influenced by a movie he'd seen about an Argentinian farmer and his son. The father had been badly injured, and the son had to run the farm on his own. It was a heavy responsibility. A wrong decision could mean losing the farm. The son decided to plant wheat. The crop thrived and the farm prospered. In the final romantic shot, the son is standing by a pile of grain, with a stunningly beautiful young woman standing opposite.

16

That made a deep impression on Milan, not just because the hero had won the love of a beautiful girl, but because his risky decision had paid off. Romance isn't just about love, it is also about following one's dream and relying on one's best instincts. And as he was pondering these things, and spinning his own dreams, his eyes would rest upon a picture that hung above the couch. The painter had depicted a peaceful winter landscape, and what impressed Milan most were the wagon tracks leading through the snow to a farmhouse. Milan always imagined this farmhouse was a mill. At that moment, all roads seemed to lead to a mill…

But Milan's childhood was not entirely idyllic. His father had many international contacts, both in England and overseas. One day, he invited an Arab businessman to his office in the sawmill. The man was a chain smoker, which had a tremendous impact on Milan, who was only four or five years old at the time. He was fascinated by how

the Arab would light each cigarette and inhale the smoke. He wanted to imitate him, but how? He solved the problem quite simply: he stole some of the cigarettes. He then crawled under the sawmill, which stood on pillars, and with the sawdust piling up around him, he lit one of the stolen cigarettes. A column of blue smoke rose through the cracks in the floor above. The workers saw the smoke and thought the mill must be on fire. All the employees rushed outside and sounded the alarm. But of course it wasn't a fire; it was little Milan sitting in the sawdust, smoking away to his heart's content. He was very convincing. He had observed very closely how the Arab did it.

When the workers saw it was Milan, they all stopped short. Milan's father walked up to his son, snatched away the cigarette, stubbed it out, lifted the little boy up, and carried him to his office.

"Now," his father ordered, in a voice that permitted no denial, "you will go to the gentleman and apologize!" He told Milan what he had to say. By this time, his mother, and everyone else, including all the employees, had gathered around the table where the Arab was sitting. He was a huge man and was clearly enjoying himself enormously. Milan burst into tears and said: "Sir, I am a thief. I stole your cigarettes, and I am very, very sorry."

It was humiliating! He looked pleadingly at his father, begging to be let go. But his father was unrelenting, and the harder Milan wept, the harder the Arab laughed.

Milan never found out whether he was laughing because he didn't understand Czech or because Milan's tearful apology amused him, but he learned a lot from that incident. It taught him one should not steal, and although he didn't realize it at the time, it also taught him to face an embarrassing situation head on and act like a man, no matter how unpleasant it might be.

FACING

Inside the sawmill in Srbeč, with Milan's father (centre left) and brother Lad'a (astride log).

The End of Childhood

APART FROM THE EPISODES with the pacifier and the stolen ciga-rettes, Milan's childhood was relatively uneventful, and he was generally happy.

The Second World War was coming to an end, but its consequences would continue to cast a dark shadow over Europe for years to come. In late 1943, the representatives of the Allied powers met in Tehran, far from the battlefields, to discuss the future of the world. President Roosevelt proposed that after the war Germany be divided into five regions, with the areas around the Kiel Canal and Hamburg, and the Ruhr and the Saar, forming two separate zones. At the Yalta Conference in early 1945, with victory in sight, Roosevelt and Churchill promised that the countries of Eastern Europe, including Czechoslovakia, would come under Stalin's sphere of influence, perhaps as a reward for the

enormous contribution the Soviet Union had made to the defeat of Nazi Germany. Thus, the fate of these countries was sealed for another forty years. The Communist parties in this region, including the Communist Party of Czechoslovakia, under the "benevolent" supervision of the Soviet Union, established their authority in one key area after another. Now and then, a train carrying Soviet soldiers would cross the border, and at one point, the Soviet government ordered the Czechoslovak government not to accept Marshall Plan aid. They did it in such an autocratic way that the popular Czechoslovak foreign minister Jan Masaryk, on his return from Moscow, would say that he had gone to Moscow as the minister of a free country and returned as Stalin's stable boy.

Events like these horrified the democratically minded in Czechoslovakia, but when you're six years old, you are barely aware of such things and see them only as an adult affair that doesn't concern you. But Milan couldn't help feeling that something strange and ominous was happening around him. In the dying days of February 1948, when the Communist leaders realized they were going to lose the next election, they staged a putsch. President Beneš, a sick and broken old man, found himself for the second time in his life in an insoluble dilemma. However desperate the situation had been in Munich in 1938, the situation in Czechoslovakia in February 1948 was even more hopeless: were he to refuse the Communist demands, he would bear the responsibility for a fratricidal civil war in which he and his supporters would remain isolated, whereas his opponents would have the might of the Soviet Union behind them. Beneš gave in and then resigned. Several days later, the body of Jan Masaryk was found under a window of his apartment in the Ministry of Foreign Affairs. To this day, the question of whether he committed suicide or was murdered has not been answered.

In September 1948, Beneš died, a broken man. The nation said farewell in what the Czech poet Jaroslav Seifert called "the month of vines, rutted roads and frozen greyness," first in a stage-managed funeral in Prague and a short time later in a small cemetery in Sezimovo Ústí. Other victims soon followed. Soldiers who had fought during the war in the British or other foreign armies were hounded down; many were arrested, and several were executed. Milada Horáková, a democratic politician who opposed the Communist takeover, was arrested and later hanged, despite international demands for clemency from people such as Einstein, Churchill, and Eleanor Roosevelt. To this day, her body has never been found. In many

FACING

Churchill, Roosevelt, and Stalin at the Yalta Conference in 1945.

LIBRARY OF CONGRESS/ DIGITAL VERSION BY SCIENCE FACTION

villages, self-appointed authorities expelled farmers from their farms and cottages. In the cities, people who refused to adapt to the new politics were thrown out of their jobs and evicted from their apartments.

In the autumn of 1948, a cloud of fear hung over the country, and the future was shrouded in uncertainty. Most children who went to school for the first time, Milan among them, did not feel anything much had changed. They did what six-year-olds usually do: chased each other, wrestled, played hide-and-seek. But Milan recalls experiencing an odd sensation the moment he entered the school building: "I don't belong here at all," he suddenly thought, and before he entered, he looked around. "Father was just backing the car away, and he stared at me with a wistful look I will never forget, as though he were saying to me, 'My boy, I hope everything will work out!'"

On that day, everything was fine. But before long, the Communists confiscated first the sawmill and then the flour mill. They let Milan's father process what was left of the grain crop, but he was not allowed to sell it. One day, on the way back home, he told Milan that he had to hand over the keys to the mill because "the Communists had taken it."

"I couldn't understand, because father had told me that one day, the mill would be mine. He tried to explain that the situation had changed and that the mill no longer belonged to us. I looked at him and shouted: 'But you promised it to me! No one else has a right to it! Take those keys and throw them in the pond!'"

Unfortunately, it was not that simple, especially as far as the mill was concerned. At the beginning at least, the Communists would sometimes pretend they were confiscating property only from people who had been accused of crimes against the Communist state.

They managed to bring a number of trumped-up charges against Milan's father, but they could find nothing to pin on his wife, who was a co-owner of the mill. When they asked her to sign off on the nationalization of the mill, she declared that three quarters of every brick in the mill belonged to her and she was not going to sign anything. The Communists harassed her for a while but then gave up and simply treated the mill as though it belonged to them anyway.

A month after his first day at school, Milan was playing with his cousin Jan by the pond:

> *Our mill was on a hill, and I saw a black Tatraplán — one of those Czech limos with the single dorsal fin at the back — crawling along the road towards us. Two men got out and two others stayed in the car. They spoke to my mother in the doorway. Even at that distance I had a feeling of anxiety that to this day I cannot explain. Then they drove away. Half an hour later they were back. This time, my father got out with them. I ran to the door, but one of the men pushed me away. "You're not allowed in there," they said, but after a while they let me enter. By this time, I knew that there was something badly wrong and I was on the verge of tears. The room was in a mess. Drawers were pulled out, their contents dumped on the floor. They were obviously looking for documents, weapons, hidden money. When they brought my father out of the bedroom, he was in handcuffs. I put my arms around his legs and clung to him and began to weep inconsolably. One of the policemen pulled me away and growled, "Stop whining! He'll come back to you." And he did come back. Almost two decades later!*

Milan's happy childhood was over.

Latin Conjugations, a Glass Eye, and Imaginary Crimes

THE COMMUNIST REGIME kept Milan's father in custody for two years before they were able to convict him. The regime did not believe in legal representation. Almost every day, they dragged him out of his cell, verbally harangued him, and tried to get him to admit to having committed some crime against the regime, which at that time had been in existence for a mere six months. His only real "crime" was that he was a capitalist, but being a capitalist was not a specific crime in the Communist criminal code, and because the Communists tried hard to create the illusion they were acting strictly according to their own laws, they could not convict Ladislav of a crime that did not exist. In the end, however, they got him — for high treason!

His "highly treasonous crime" was a simple act of kindness. Before the 1948 February putsch, Ladislav had loaned a considerable sum of money to Jiři Fikrt, the son of a friend and a former employee in the Ministry of Foreign Trade. Jiři was preparing to leave for the United States, where he planned to set up a factory to manufacture fine chinaware. His fiancée had refused to go with him at first, so following the putsch, Jiři came back to get her. They arrested him at the border. During his interrogation, Jiři admitted that Milan's father had lent him the money to finance his new business venture. Ladislav was sentenced to twenty-five years in prison. He spent the longest stretch in Leopoldov Prison, an old fortress built at the time of the Austro-Hungarian monarchy that had the same kind of reputation as Alcatraz, meaning it was almost impossible to escape from, though a handful had managed it, including a man called Pravomil Raichl, from a family who were virtually next-door neighbours of the Kroupas.

Milan's father was eventually released on January 6, 1960, after twelve years, as part of an amnesty. But it was not his last taste of prison life. During the Prague Spring, in 1968, Milan's irrepressible father started a new business, and after the Soviet invasion, he was convicted of "illegal business dealings" and sent to jail for another five years.

Despite his father's imprisonment, Milan's life at the flour mill with his mother and brother continued more or less smoothly. But his mother's life changed fundamentally. The hardest thing she had to deal with must have been a feeling of abandonment. She had once enjoyed a full social life with her husband, but now she was alone, with two growing boys; her friends had worries of their own, and they were afraid of the regime, which took a dim view of people who maintained contact with families of political prisoners. Moreover, she couldn't stop worrying about her husband. She tried to be stoic about her fate, but she knew nothing good would come from the regime, and there were moments when she was choked with sheer rage over the barbarity of its conduct towards people.

Milan witnessed one such moment. One day, he and his mother went to Leopoldpov to visit his father. She was allowed four visits a year, the boys only once a year. They arrived at seven o'clock in the morning and waited outside the gate to be let in. Milan remembers exactly what happened next.

"One of the guards came out and spoke to my mother: 'So, did you bring the glass eye?' the guard said. My mother shuddered. 'Glass eye?' 'You mean you don't know your husband lost an eye?' Mother burst into tears, and the guard said he'd go and check. Naturally, Father hadn't lost an eye. It was just a cruel joke the guards played on prisoners' wives."

For the first five or six years, they got by selling the gold Milan's father had bought in better times, which they'd managed to keep hidden from the Communists. When the gold ran out, they sold the farmhouse (owning a small dwelling was still permitted), along with the orchards and gardens around it. Then his mother found work turning wheat in the fields at harvest time so that it would dry properly. She found a second job binding books in Prague, and ended up working in Slaný as a bricklayer's assistant. She would return home each evening after seven and then would have to tend to the household. There was little time left to look after the two boys.

Shortly after the putsch, the Communists moved three other families into the mill. One of them was a woman Milan called "Auntie," who would look after him occasionally, particularly in winter. One especially cold winter's day at the mill, he went without his skates to play hockey on the pond. The ice was usually not very thick, and he

had already broken through several times and ended up in water up to his neck. His mother was terrified, but her attempts to stop him were in vain. On that day, Milan remembers, he was on the pond watching a tractor going by, when the ice broke again and in he plunged. He crawled out, soaked to the skin, and ran home. By the time he got there, his clothing was frozen solid. Auntie got him out of his clothes, and he crawled under a warm duvet. Around seven, his mother came back from work. Milan pretended to be asleep. He heard Auntie tell his mother he wasn't feeling well, but his mother saw the wet clothes on the line, and before he knew it, she had pulled the covers off him

and, holding the duvet in one hand, grabbed a whip from the wall and gave him a thrashing. Milan gave up playing hockey and took up soccer. Soccer was safer, if only because there was no danger of falling through the ice.

When he was in grade nine, his mother transferred him to a school in Slaný, for two reasons: the school was better, and he could live with his uncle. His uncle was strict, and if there was something Milan sorely needed, it was discipline and paternal authority. He enjoyed soccer far more than Latin conjugations, but his uncle believed that proficiency in Latin was more important. Once, just before a soccer practice, he asked Milan what they were studying in Latin at the moment. They were studying declensions, he replied. His uncle asked him to demonstrate what he had learned. Milan didn't do very well, so his uncle sent him upstairs to his room to learn the declensions properly. "When you've learned them you can go to practice."

Milan wasn't good at it, but his desire to go to soccer practice was so great that after his uncle's third visit to his room, he had learned the declensions to his uncle's satisfaction. To this day, Milan still remembers them.

This lesson gave him a firmer grasp of Latin but also taught him something far more valuable: nothing in life comes without effort. Today, when he looks at the younger generation, he has the impression they are essentially no worse than his own, but because they don't have to fight as hard for what they want, they are certainly softer. Looking back, he sees that his parents did the best they could for him, but he also knows that their best, in a material sense, was less than the best he's been able to provide for his own children. His parents' limitations, however, were not necessarily a bad thing. Even his father's imprisonment and the confiscation of the family property forced Milan to fight his way through life, to get the things he wanted through his own efforts. If his own children wanted something, they simply went out and bought it.

Milan accepts what fate dealt him. Although many might consider the circumstances of his childhood tragic, he would change nothing about his life. Except perhaps for the episode with the Christmas tree, which we will learn about in Chapter 8.

Goal Keeper and Lathe Operator... Almost

IN GRADE EIGHT, Milan began taking a more active interest in soccer. On his way home from school with the boys, they would stop somewhere in a meadow, and one of them always had a soccer ball with him. They would divide into two teams and start playing. What battles they were!

He went to grammar school from 1953 to 1955. Since he was "an undesirable political element," the authorities banned him from going any further. At that time, Milan wasn't much interested in books, but the ban also meant he couldn't do what he really wanted, which was to study at a mill workers' vocational school and take over the family mill, which the regime had, for all practical, if not legal, purposes, confiscated. The problem was that the local Communists didn't know what to do with the mill, so they permitted Milan's family, with a single mill hand, to continue operating it under party supervision. Milan got along very well with the mill hand, whose name was Laďa Hrazdil. Hrazdil patiently taught him how to sift the ground flour into varying degrees of coarseness and manage the machinery. Milan was a good student: "I did very well. What I liked most of all was that it was a huge mill with a lot of machines, and eventually, I knew how to run them all."

His delight did not last long:

On one occasion, the bosses of the Central Bohemian Flour Mills enterprise came for an inspection. The mill hand happened to have the flu, so I was in charge of running the place. At first, the big cheeses made fun of me, but when they learned that the employee was off sick and I was running the mill on my own, there was hell to pay. "What was this Hrazdil thinking? Letting this capitalist brat work here on his own!" I was fifteen years old. I had to shut the mill down and put a seal on the door, and then we went to get the mill hand. We did an inventory with him, and it turned out we had a five-hundred-kilo surplus. They accused us of holding it back to sell privately, which was not allowed at that time.

Very shortly after that, people from the local farm cooperative approached my mother and urged her to join, saying that they were going to train me as a tractor driver. By my sixteenth year, I would have qualified for my driver's licence. Mum told them that I was away at a soccer training camp and that I was playing for the junior division of the Kladno sports club. That impressed them. The minute they heard that I was good at sports, the fact that I was a "capitalist brat" didn't bother them as much.

Although under the Communist system everyone is allegedly equal (everyone had the same title: Comrade Marshal, Comrade Janitor, Comrade Hangman), the reality was a little different: citizens who were skilled at kicking soccer balls were given advantages denied those who were not good at kicking anything. The regime was clearly aware that young men dream of being famous, going out with pretty girls, and making lots of money, so they allowed them to realize these dreams through sport. The regime was also aware, as the rulers of ancient Rome had been, that people need circuses as well as bread, and that what they were offering — parades on May Day and Armed Forces Day, celebrations of super-productivity — were not very entertaining,

Milan's grade eight class. Milan is in the first row, third from the right.

so they allowed large state enterprises to run their own sports clubs, mostly soccer clubs, and to attract players from other clubs by offering them non-egalitarian perks.

Milan began to play soccer seriously in his thirteenth year:

I came to it in a very odd way. Once during phys. ed. class, we were doing the long jump. I couldn't jump far enough, so I decided to do a somersault when I was jumping. In that way, I broke my own record, even though I fell on my butt. In short, I always looked for a way to stand out, even though it may have been unorthodox. I also learned that I really enjoyed a spontaneous and unplanned way of moving, and it occurred to me that this is the kind of movement that goalies have to cultivate. So, during soccer training sessions and matches, I began to jump after the ball like a monkey and to react in unusual ways in unforeseen situations.

Milan didn't need a lot of persuasion to take up soccer. Among other things, this was because he was able to be what they called, in the sports jargon of the time, "a productive player," and he drew attention to himself, because, as he says, "on a soccer team there's only one goalie, and if he's good, he's the hero."

Fortunately, Milan was driven by more than just a boyish desire to be cock of the walk. There was always a pragmatic core to his behaviour, a focus on the practical things in life. As he stood in the goal — during moments when the action was at the other end of the pitch and there was no immediate danger the ball would come flying at him — he realized this was a magnificent opportunity to analyze the way players on the opposing team played, how they kicked, how they dribbled, and how they passed the ball. It was also an opportunity to study his own team, mainly the defence but the other players as well.

This practice would come in very handy in the future — at that point still a long way off — when he would observe and analyze his employees as they did their work.

When the cooperative farm approached his mother about joining the organization and training him as a tractor driver, Milan was playing for the junior division of the Kladno sports club, but he was also being scouted by a rival club, čKD Slaný, where a friend of his father's, a builder called Hyke, had considerable influence. It was certainly thanks to Hyke that čKD told Milan if he ever wanted to come over to the junior division of their club, they would take him. Milan accepted the offer, and the offer of a job with the čKD engineering firm that went with it, and for a moment, he felt himself to be the centre of the universe. And why not? He was a young, sturdy, good-looking goalie in the junior division of a good team — its youngest member, in fact. Despite the repugnant regime running the country, Milan's life seemed full of the promise of fame, fortune, and yes, beautiful women.

Milan has always liked women, and they have always been drawn to him. Not that it always turned out well. He noticed (and this began to have a particularly powerful impact on him when he began to play for a premier league team) that when his teammates came on to the field, they came in accompanied by a woman: a wife, fiancée, or pretty girlfriend. At the next important match, which was against his old team, Kladno, he walked onto the field with a beautiful girl on his arm. "I was so distracted that I forgot what I was doing," Milan says. "I let in six goals, and on the bus on the way home I swore I would never again allow myself to be carried away by the superficial glow of celebrity."

A commendable resolution in someone so young, but this young man already knew there was something he wanted, even though at the time he didn't know precisely what it was.

"I also realized how important it was to be able to look myself frankly in the eye, make no excuses, and acknowledge my mistakes… to always have a sensitive radar, to always be willing to look for, and risk, taking a different route."

Did Milan really realize this with so much clarity at such a young age, or was this wisdom merely the seed of an idea he later nurtured into full flower in struggles with himself? But we're already anticipating a time when Milan was able to shape — as far as circumstances allowed — his own destiny. Before we get to his final, almost fantastic, soccer episode in his native country, however, we must say a few words about Milan as a lathe operator.

When he was eighteen, a lathe operator in the boiler room of the ČKD factory retired. Milan told his boss he wanted to fill the man's position. His boss replied he would get the job, but only after he'd finished his compulsory military service. Milan replied that he wanted the job "right now." Confident, stubborn, and defiant, Milan was someone who stood on principle. In this case, the principle was outstanding in its simplicity: what Milan wants, Milan gets. The fact that this discussion was taking place in a country ruled over, though in a somewhat milder form than a decade earlier, by a brutal dictatorship whose leaders handed out orders and punished disobedience harshly, played practically no role at all in Milan's decision-making. The most he was willing to admit was that the regime (in this case represented by his boss) was an opponent against whom it was interesting to measure his strength.

His response to his boss's refusal was to sit at his lathe with his hands in his lap. That angered the boss's superior, who yelled at Milan to get back to work. This shook Milan's self-confidence a little, since he realized they could send him to prison, so he began to subtly change his position: instead of refusing to work, he said if they didn't give him the job in the boiler room, he would no longer work as a lathe operator; instead, he would do anything else they asked of him. So they made him a driver's mate, responsible for collecting the metal filings and carting them off to the scrap processor. It was a great job, because it allowed Milan to drive through the entire factory, talk about soccer to his fellow workers, and bask in their admiration for his tremendous goal-keeping skills. He had a very good time, but for understandable reasons, the top boss did not like this, so he transferred Milan to the steel-tempering division, after which they transferred him several more times. Milan knew they were testing

39

him and that, should he refuse to work at any of those jobs, they would lock him up.

In the end, he was summoned to a meeting with the trade union. The trade union reps were sitting in a circle with an empty chair in the middle. Milan sat down. He has never forgotten what followed: "After opening the meeting, the chairman accused me of being work-shy. I replied that it wasn't true, that wherever they sent me I had worked to the best of my ability. It's just that I didn't want to be a lathe operator anywhere else but in the boiler room. After all, I had the right to freely decide what I wanted to do."

Talk of freedom was practically blasphemy, and the chairman replied: "Do you realize that we have invested twenty-five thousand crowns in you, despite the fact that your father is a convicted capitalist, your mother is a capitalist, and you're a capitalist brat?" (Clearly they were all singing from the same ideological hymnbook.) "Your parents brought you up very badly indeed."

"'If I'd listened to my parents,' I replied, 'I would have been a lathe operator, but I'm eighteen years old, and my parents can't tell me what to do. Leave them out of this! This is my decision. You say you spent twenty-five thousand crowns on me? Here, take what you see in the palm of my hand!' And I held out my empty hand. The chairman raised his arm as though he were about to slap my face, then he stopped himself, looked around at the other comrades, spat, then left the room. The upshot was that I was immediately dropped from the soccer team."

Milan's struggle with the regime continued during his military service, which he began with the engineering corps in Bratislava. They did their military drills on a soccer field. One early evening, when he was walking around the barracks, Milan heard a referee's whistle, which drew him the way the children of Hanover were drawn to the Pied Piper. It led him towards his destiny, which in Milan's case meant the soccer field.

> *The boys were dressed in smart uniforms, and the coach was putting them through their paces. I watched the practice session with excitement and regret. They were very good at scrimmages. Finally, I plucked up my courage, went up to the coach, and said, "Could I play with you?"*
>
> *The coach asked what position I played and I told him that I was a goalie and he put me in goal for a while. When the drills were over he came up to me and said: "Man, how did you get here in the first place? Of course, we'll put you on the team." And what team was that? Dukla Bratislava, one of the top teams in the city. That made my time in the army very enjoyable, although it was not all smooth sailing.*
>
> *Once, after a big match, I was tired and fell asleep on sentry duty. At 5 AM, the major knocked on the window of the guardhouse and said, "Private, you're going to the brig!" I expected them to take me away, but eventually the coach and the captain of the team came and said: "Well, normally there would be hell to pay for this, but I explained to the comrade major here that we had a game yesterday, and I told him what an effort you'd put out and that boys like you who really give their all shouldn't have to do sentry duty. So you're off the hook."*

And thus was the Communist principle of the equality of all comrades famously upheld.

Military Life

NOT LONG BEFORE Milan began his military service, his father was released from prison. He came home in the summer of Milan's eighteenth year. At that time, Milan thought of his father as something between a god and Superman. He expected that with his father's return everything would change; they would have a car again and could go back to living the life they led before the Communists took over. None of that happened. Life continued to be just as grey as it had been during the long years of his father's imprisonment.

Milan reacted to his father's return with what, years later, he would describe as the naive cruelty of youth: "No car miraculously appeared. Mum continued working late into the night, and our lives did not change. When Christmas came, I lost my last little bit of hope. I remember us all sitting around the Christmas tree. I looked at the

modest presents, then looked at my mother: 'You know, Mum, we had better Christmases when Dad wasn't here.'"

"That is one moment in my life that I would give anything to be able to take back," Milan says. "Dad was standing beside the Christmas tree with his head down, and he didn't say a word. Not only did he not react to what I'd said, but he never held it against me, and he never mentioned it again. I didn't realize it at the time, but at that moment he was a real Superman."

Before Milan enlisted, he began to learn German and discovered he was good at it. His father supported his efforts, because he couldn't see a future for Milan in Czechoslovakia. To improve his German skills, Milan visited Dresden in the DDR three times. Milan's cohort — the group of men born in 1943 — was called up by the army two months early. The Berlin Wall was going up, and it felt like a mobilization for war. His company was sent to Bratislava to join a bridge-building unit. They were taken to the base. The officer who received Milan was holding a sheaf of personnel reports in his hand, and growled: "Hmm, Kroupa, seems you're a bit work-shy. Well, we'll knock that out of you."

Following this welcome, they had to stand on the parade ground for several hours, and Milan became very thirsty. There was a water tap a few steps away from where he stood, but he wasn't allowed to use it. That was when it sank in. Yesterday, he could have gone to the tap and had a drink; today, for the first time in his life, he was experiencing the helplessness of a virtual prisoner, the helplessness his father must have felt during his long years in prison.

His German served him very well in the army. There was a platoon of Sudeten Germans at the camp who had finished their two-year stint but were forced to stay on because of the political situation. As Milan was the only person there who could speak German, they took him under their wing.

Every morning, the recruits had classes in civics that extolled the miraculous achievements of Communism. He found that particularly hard to take, given what he knew about the miraculous achievements of Communism. After a time, he was selected to go to Štúrovo, in southeastern Slovakia, to learn to drive trucks. In Štúrovo, he met many Hungarians who had never forgotten that the Czechs and Slovaks had failed to come to their assistance during the Hungarian uprising against the Communists in 1956. Štúrovo had some minor inconveniences — the base lacked even rudimentary latrines. The facilities consisted of a board where everyone had to sit side by side and watch each other doing their business. Milan found this intolerable. He had to have privacy. So when nature called, he would wait until dark, jump over the barbed wire, and squat in the grass.

One night, a sentry shone a flashlight at him and shouted (sometimes they shot first): "What are you doing there?"

Milan replied bravely: "Can't you see?"

The sentry could not see and ordered Milan to stand up.

"I can't. I shit my pants."

The sentry took it philosophically. "So wipe your ass and get over here."

As a command to be obeyed it was a model of practical advice, and Milan complied.

Towards the end of his stint, there was a serious diarrhea outbreak on the base. As one of the few unaffected soldiers, Milan was ordered to help in the kitchen. He was terribly bored. In desperation, he pretended to have a sore throat and was sent to the infirmary. The doctor was disappointed; he may have expected something more inventive in the way of a feigned illness. He dipped a swab onto a tincture of iodine and stuck it deep into Milan's throat. It stung so painfully Milan felt he was about to die. The doctor was pleased with himself. "There you are!" he said dryly. "Now you really do have a sore throat!"

In the infirmary, Milan met Franta, who would become his best friend and remains so to this day. They celebrated together when Milan got his truck operator's licence. The celebration lasted only a few days, since Milan was then released to return to the barracks. He organized his next foray into the infirmary by claiming he had rheumatism. The reunion with Franta had to take place in the infirmary because their plan was to pick up nurses. If there was no movie being shown on the base, they would take them to the movies in town. The only problem was that the seats there squeaked very loudly.

Three weeks later, when they were both released from the infirmary, the two friends, after some thought, concluded it would be a great pity — practically a sin — to go straight back to the barracks. They decided to take a brief leave of absence and went into town. They didn't return to the barracks until 3 AM. The military police were waiting for them, and they were ordered to report to their superior officer. Milan remembers him as "the little captain," a small man whose size clearly gave the psychological advantage to Milan, who is six feet tall. As they approached him, Milan whispered, "Franta, listen to what I say, and then say the same thing to the little captain."

"What was the idea of wandering about the city like that until morning?" the captain barked.

Adopting a contrite tone, which over time he had cultivated to a level of classic perfection, Milan replied: "You know, Comrade Captain, we never really thought very much about it. We get out so seldom that we were simply unaware that it was an offence to show up late. I know we made a mistake. It won't happen again."

The little captain ate it up. He gave Milan a conciliatory nod and said, "Dismissed!"

Milan left the captain's office but waited outside the door, listening. Franta was supposed to make an identical excuse, but instead, being one of the few people in the world who speaks the truth in every circumstance, Franta dropped a bomb on the captain: "Well, we saw our chance and we took it," he said.

Immediately afterwards, Milan heard the chair fall over as the captain shot out of his seat, and then he heard his thundering voice: "You had your chance yesterday. I've got mine today!"

"They sent Franta to the brig," Milan says. "I was on the other side of the door, and I pretended I didn't hear anything. When Franta walked past me, he gave me a disgusted look and growled: 'You son of a bitch!' He had to serve two weeks behind bars. One day, I was walking past the barracks and I saw a large hole. Every once in a while, a little bit of clay would come flying out of it. There was a guard standing next to it. I looked down and there was Franta with a shovel. Franta looked up and blurted out, 'You son of a bitch!' And we're still the best of friends."

48

Destiny in the Palm of One's Hand

MILAN'S MOTHER BELIEVED there is a world beyond us and there are people who know how to make contact with that world. She believed in spiritual healers. She was also heavily influenced by a story her husband told. When he was eighteen, he suddenly went blind. His parents took him to see many doctors, but none could say what had caused the blindness. About two months later, his vision spontaneously returned. Many years later (by this time, he was already married), he came down with acute bronchitis. The famous spiritual healer Koči (who, according to Milan, "accurately predicted his own death down to the last detail") cured him by placing his hand on Milan's father's forehead. And when he became ill again — by now he was in prison — Milan's mother went to Prague to see Koči and bought a photograph of his palm from him, which her husband then pressed to the place where he was experiencing pain. It gave him immediate relief. His father's religious disposition may have had something to do with it. When Milan asked him how he had managed to survive long stretches in solitary confinement, he replied: "It was my faith in God."

During her husband's incarceration, Milan's mother gathered together a circle of female spiritualists who regularly met at the mill. She also began to do automatic drawings, convinced that her hand was guided by a supernatural power. As an adolescent, Milan always had to wait outside, sometimes for an hour, while the leading clairvoyant was speaking. He would never have admitted it — it would have been beneath his adolescent dignity — but he did not take these seances lightly, perhaps sensing there were many interesting things between heaven and earth that we know nothing of. Much later, when he began to think more deeply about these phenomena, he would explain his belief roughly as follows:

I imagine that we are driving a car and the windshield is painted over in black. When we look into the rearview mirror, we see the past. If we are driving fast, we barely register the present. But we have absolutely no way of seeing the future we're speeding towards. Our reactions cannot be based on rational thought. Intuition is the only thing that can help us, and the ability to connect with the higher principles of the future.

Then Milan went on to contradict himself:

There are exceptional people who do have the gift of seeing the future. I believe we all have this gift of clairvoyance, but not all of us work to develop it. All we need to do is wipe the windscreen clean. But how? Our disadvantage is that we depend on our five senses. We don't trust anything that deviates from what those senses tell us, and therefore we don't trust ourselves. Energies or beings may exist around us that we can't touch and can't see. Does that mean that they don't exist? Radio waves exist, but we can't hear them without a receiver, and we can't hear a high-pitched whistle that a dog can hear either.

Milan may have been intrigued by these seances because he subconsciously sensed fate had special plans for him. Once, when he was about fifteen, he went into the living room after the seance was over to get a glass of water. The clairvoyant was still sitting on her chair, and when Milan walked past she stopped him: "Come here! Would you like me to tell you something about your future?"

Because he didn't quite know how to respond, Milan nodded. The fortune-teller took him by the hand and examined his palm. For a long time, she seemed perplexed by what she saw there, and when she finally spoke, she seemed almost embarrassed: "You're somewhere far away. I see a puddle… a pond… no, it's the sea. You are going to travel over the ocean."

Milan thought that was highly unlikely:

I said to myself, "Right, that's the first bit of nonsense. I won't be travelling over any ocean."

Then she said, "I see you driving a large vehicle. I think it's a truck. I see you're going to have a lot of trouble with girls. I can also see what you'll be doing with your life. What would you like to know, about your future jobs or about the girls?"

Well, what do you think I said? I was fifteen… "About the girls!" I said. "Girls will be your weakness," she said. "You're going to have a lot of problems… I see black hair…"

Today, I have to admit that she described in some detail one of my great loves, and I did have major problems with her on this side of the pond.

Milan's trouble with girls began when he was seventeen. In Dřetovice at the time, there was a young woman called Marie, who was four years older than Milan. One evening, they fell into a friendly conversation, and to impress Marie, Milan tried to come across as an experienced Don Juan, regaling her with colourful but imaginary accounts of his escapades with women. She probably didn't believe him, but still, either because it excited her or because she wanted to call his bluff, she egged him on. Milan recalls the moment when his virginity was on the line:

Before I knew what was happening, Marie invited me to act. She lay on her back, and I saw miraculous things I'd never seen before. I looked around and whispered to myself, "Boys, help me out here!" I'd never felt a greater need to have my soccer team around. But I was on my own, and even though I was a rank amateur, I managed to score a goal. Marie looked at me askance, dusted herself off, and said: "Well, Milan, I can see that I've got a lot to teach you." I was thrilled. But despite my frequent efforts, I was never able to score in that particular goal again.

After Marie came the pretty Slovak girl Růženka, about whom we will hear more in Chapter 11.

Another story, one with a certain ideological charm, comes from the time when Milan worked in a factory that made prefabricated panels for apartment buildings. Most of the employees were women, and all of them were members of a Communist organization called the Czechoslovak Union of Youth (ČSM). These women took a shine to Milan and came to him with a subversive suggestion: "Come and join the union. We need a new chairman. We'll elect you chairman, and you can come on holiday with us."

"At first I hesitated," Milan recalls. "But in the end, I found their offer irresistible. Besides, one of them, a blonde, was very attractive. So I applied to join, and I, a capitalist brat, became chairman of a branch of the youth union. At the time, they picked the twenty most worthy members to go on a summer outing to the Tatra Mountains in Slovakia. As chairman, I was guaranteed a place. All expenses were paid, and the holiday was perfect. We went on hikes together through the Tatras, and in the evenings we had great fun."

But nothing lasts forever. "When we got back from the Tatras, the chairman of the trade union called me into his office and started

Milan (right) on the trip to the Tatra Mountains in Slovakia, as chair of the local branch of the Czechoslovak Union of Youth.

yelling at me. To tell you the truth, I wasn't surprised. How could I have dared, as a capitalist brat, to become chairman of the Czechoslovak Union of Youth?"

Milan replied bravely: "'You see, Comrade Chairman, since the members of the Czechoslovak Union of Youth recruited me, they must have seen something in me.'" Comrade Chairman completely lost it. He turned as red as a turkey's wattle and shouted, 'I'll tell you what they saw in you! Shit is what they saw in you!' As he was yelling, the intensity of his voice weakened until he became completely hoarse."

Seen from a distance, and completely without prejudice, this story must have hastened the end of the Communist regime by at least half an hour.

It was about this time Milan began to think seriously about leaving Czechoslovakia. He found a job as a driver with the Prague Institute of Hematology and Blood Transfusion. He'd barely settled in, though, when the "trouble with girls" started again. In fact, it wasn't really his fault. It's just that he kept realizing again and again how wonderful it was to be young and have no obligations. And life was on his side. When he landed a job in Prague, he needed lodgings. One day he was driving along Ruská Street when he saw a rather frail old lady trying to unlock the door to her apartment. He stopped to help her and she offered him a room in her apartment. Now that he had a place to stay, he had more time for his favourite pastime, and he devoted himself to it wholeheartedly. Every weekend he took a girl home with him to Dřetovice — a different one each time.

One of them was called Míša. She was a ballerina in the national the-atre, and she had contacts abroad. Milan saw her as a friend who would help him find a way out of the country. But Míša fell in love with Milan. She managed to obtain invitations, required by law, for both of them to go to Paris (this was one small indication the Communist regime was relaxing its hold a little). She hoped they could escape and make a life together. Milan saw it differently: "When I saw that there were two separate invitations, one for each of us, I threw hers out and only used my own."

It was a swinish thing to do, even though Milan was probably not entirely aware of that at the time. It was a long time ago, and he could easily have swept it under the rug. Would anyone know about it today? The point is, Milan Kroupa knows about it, and in talking about it, he confirmed again that conscience is something that remains with us until death.

"To this day, I regret what I did. I betrayed a friend who had fallen in love with me and believed we had a future together." Milan Kroupa has come a long way in forty years.

But of all the women he met, it was Milena who had the deepest and most lasting impact on his life. He first saw her when he and Franta, his army buddy, were sitting in the Speciál bar, which at the time was on Na Přikopech near the Powder Tower in Prague. Franta gave Milan a conspiratorial look and said: "Take a look at that girl over there. She's gorgeous. No makeup! A natural beauty!"

Milan looked at her and replied: "Are you out of your mind? She can't be more than fourteen or fifteen. She's jail bait."

What Milan didn't tell Franta was the beautiful young woman was sitting with one of his former girlfriends, and when Franta went home to change his clothes, Milan sat down with the two girls and went to work. By the time Franta returned, Milan knew the young woman was eighteen, six years younger than Milan, and her name was Milena (practically an anagram of his own name). He also knew he'd fallen madly in love with her.

When he first took Milena home to the mill in Dřetovice, his father took him to one side: "This one is different. This one you can get serious about."

10

In the Glow of Millions

AS HE WAS GROWING UP, Milan began to realize that life's journey is determined not only by circumstances but also by character. He began to think about the lessons his father was teaching him. He began to see the world from a broader perspective. He began to think about how we make decisions:

> When we're at a fork in the road, we can go either one way or the other. If we take the proper road, things go well. If we choose the wrong road, we discover that we have to change course in order to succeed. The most important thing is not to be afraid to make a decision, to step out and embrace a goal. That was always part of my nature, and it still is.

When I invest my time in something, I'm reluctant to let it go. In my case, ego has also played a large role. I hate to admit defeat. Ego is a double-edged sword. We can use it to our benefit or to our detriment. We have to be willing to admit our mistakes. It's like that fiasco with the girl at the soccer match, when I was trying to impress her and instead let in six goals: if I hadn't been able to admit that I had done something stupid, and had looked for excuses instead, I'd have never progressed beyond that point. Positive ego demands a very strict sense of responsibility regarding one's own abilities. A negative ego is nothing more than a desire to look good in front of others.

His father knew there was no future for Milan in Czechoslovakia, so he prepared him to be able to adapt to any circumstance that might present itself. He told him about his own beginnings in business, about what motivated some of his actions — making paintbrush handles from scrap wood, for instance, which he then exported to England. He taught Milan practical things, such as how to determine whether there was enough water in the mill track to drive the turbine: "You measure the width and the depth of the river. Then you take a blade of grass, throw it into the current, and time how long it takes it to go a hundred metres," Milan explains.

"What fascinated me," Milan says today, "was this combination of mathematics, vision, and down-to-earth common sense. That, in a nutshell, is the most precious thing that my father gave me. However, on one occasion there wasn't enough water and the turbines did not turn, and I pointed out to him that he hadn't done the math. We both had a good laugh."

His father filled Milan's heart and soul with indelible impressions, the kind that stay with us for the rest of our lives, most of all in moments when the world seems overwhelming. He remembers that

Milan's father in Prague, 1960.

the only livestock they were permitted to keep was a pig, so every year they had a traditional slaughtering party. He also remembers how he and his father made cinder blocks using waste from the blast furnaces in the Kladno steel mill:

Once, father brought home some cinder block forms. I don't know where he found them. My brother didn't want anything to do with it, but I really enjoyed it. We could make four cinder blocks at once. Dad's plan was that when we had enough to build a house, we would sell them. These were some of the happiest moments of my youth, when I was working beside my father and we would talk. It never occurred to me to ask for money. I really enjoyed seeing the blocks accumulate, and I was fascinated by the system. You made concrete from the slag and ash from the steel mills, then poured the concrete into the form, closed it, and shook it for a while so that the concrete would settle and there would be no air bubbles in it. When the cinder blocks had dried, the form was lifted off and the whole process began again.

The episode with the cinder blocks taught Milan something else: children of the same parents can be very different. For Milan, making those blocks with his father was something pleasurable and creative, but his brother, Ladislav, didn't enjoy it at all and thought his father was crazy. His attitude angered their father so much that he once went after Ladislav with a shovel. He raised it, then realized what he was doing, and slowly lowered it. "You and I are finished here," he said finally.

Milan was, and still is, particularly grateful to his father for one gift, a novel by František Sokol-Tůma, banned at the time, called *In the Glow of Millions*. Milan's first reaction was not particularly positive:

It had five sections in two modestly sized volumes. Up to that point, I had almost never read an entire book, and so I ignored it at first. I thought Father was naive to think that I was suddenly going to start reading, but I didn't want to argue with him. So I took the books and casually put them at the back of the table. But as usual, Father's words stayed with me: "You should read this. It might interest you. And you might get something out of it."

"In the Glow of Millions! *What a stupid title! Who cares about millions?" I said to myself stubbornly. But it was almost impossible to ignore these two little volumes. It was as though they were staring at me from the corner of the room. Once I came in and caught sight of the familiar covers, and it suddenly occurred to me that I was being ungrateful. Did I think that at the age of eighteen I'd absorbed all the wisdom in the world?* "Father means well. He's trying to help you. He took the risk of getting you a forbidden book, and you don't even have the decency to look at it and decide whether it's worth reading or not." *I also knew that Dad would certainly ask me whether I had read it, and so I really had no choice. Somewhat reluctantly, I picked up the first volume.*

Just reading the introduction made me feel excited. After the second chapter, you couldn't have torn me away. Even so, it took me about a month to read both volumes. It was the fascinating story of an entrepreneur at the end of the nineteenth century in the Ostrava region and Poland, who had created a successful business out of nothing and then gone bankrupt. After the bankruptcy, however, he refused to give up. When his business collapsed around him like a ruined building, he patiently picked up the pieces and created the framework of a new business. Each failure taught him something new. He refused to give up. There's a perfect expression for this in English: "Failure is not an option."

Many people read things that inspire them at first, but then they cool off. I think the key to my success was that I completely identified with this story. I really felt for the hero. At the time, I was not so interested in the national and racial conflicts described in the book, nor in the cruelty and the ruthlessness of the hero's actions. What got my attention was how clever and determined he was.

The result was that I was fired up with the idea of any kind of business enterprise. I understood the basic conditions for success. You might even say that I divide my approach to learning into two periods: before In the Glow of Millions *and after* In the Glow of Millions. *In the first period, I learned things only because I had to. Father pushed me hard to take private German lessons, which I took seriously. But after reading the book, I began to study with great gusto, because it was clear that Father was right when he told me: "This regime is not for you. You're going to have to leave." Unlike my brother, Lad'a, whom Father worried was adapting to the regime, he saw in me a spark that he patiently nourished until it caught fire and ignited my own internal flame. That little book shifted me out of my youthful lethargy when I was only interested in girls and soccer. I said to myself: "Father was right: if you ever want to experience something like that, you really will have to leave the country." From that moment on, I began to seriously prepare for my exit.*

Růženka

ONE OF THE MANY THINGS Milan owes to his father is the fact that he arranged for him to study German. Milan took to German easily, but over the course of three trips to Dresden, he discovered although he could speak German fairly well, he had trouble understanding it. However, travel to a country where German was spoken, and where he could quickly improve his language skills, was not easy, not even for an excellent soccer player like Milan. "As the son of a capitalist family, I was not allowed to go to matches in the West. I could only travel with the team to matches in the Eastern Bloc," Milan says. Even though the regime was far from being as arrogantly overbearing as it had been in the beginning, it was still a long way from collapse.

The victory over Hitler, and the meeting between Churchill, Roosevelt, and Stalin at Yalta towards the end of the war, confirmed the dominant position of the Soviet Union in Eastern and Central Europe for the foreseeable future, though perhaps not forever, as Communist propaganda proclaimed on the airwaves every day. The regime tried to control all aspects of life: economic, political, religious, and military, and for a while it seemed as though it was unshakeable — but things began to shift. Only a few short years after their military and diplomatic victory, the Communists launched an internal power struggle. In Czechoslovakia, this struggle took the form of the notorious trials of Rudolf Slanský and others, in all likelihood directed by Moscow, in which fourteen of the accused were found guilty of treason, and Slanský and ten others were sentenced to death. Slanský was executed on December 3, 1952, but eleven years later, the same regime exonerated him, and in 1968, he was posthumously reinstated as a member of the party.

In the Soviet Union, almost at the same time, Stalin's health became worse, and at the end of February 1953, he fell into a coma from which he never recovered.

Slanský's trial and Stalin's death were two events that undermined the self-confidence of that murderous regime. I don't know how much attention Milan paid to these events, though the Hungarian uprising in 1956 must have made an impression on him. In the main, he was absorbed in his own life and, when the time came, in his army service.

The reader will remember that Private Kroupa spent his army days in Bratislava, and while walking through the barracks early one evening, he heard the sound of a whistle that drew him to a soccer field where the coach was putting the players through their paces. That encounter ended auspiciously, with Milan becoming the goaltender for Dukla Bratislava.

But that wasn't the end of it. This is how Milan remembers his Bratislava debut:

We were constantly surrounded by a bevy of young women. I got to know a very pretty Slovak girl called Růženka, and we started going out together. It was a carefree romance, but one day we were out walking and she told me that she was pregnant. I thought that my reaction was wonderfully responsible: "Don't worry about it," I said. "I'll take care of it. Have it dealt with and I'll pay for everything."

It was a simple solution — on Milan's part.

But Růženka didn't see it that way. She wouldn't hear of an abortion. She said she'd have the child on her own, and because I could just imagine what my father would say, I began to lose it. I had no idea what to do, but I was certain that there would be hell to pay at home. I went through a classic nervous breakdown. My superiors recommended that I see a psychiatrist. I found myself in the same hospital where I'd recently gone for a sore throat and rheumatism. An older doctor came to me and asked, in a sympathetic tone: "So, what's the problem here? What could possibly be so serious that you've tied your nerves in a knot?"

I told him I'd made a girl pregnant and that my father would kill me and probably wouldn't survive himself. The doctor was completely unruffled. "Everything will sort itself out, you'll see. We'll give you a thirteen-day leave. Go home and explain everything to your parents. Just don't worry. Everything will be fine."

Milan went home, but he dithered, and before he knew it, there was only one day left in his leave and he still hadn't said a word to his parents. On the thirteenth day, his mother told Milan she was going into the village to do some shopping. Milan offered to go with her. The village was about two kilometres away, and as they were walking along a narrow path through a beautiful meadow, Milan's mother suddenly stopped and looked him in the eye. "You've got someone pregnant," she said matter-of-factly. When Milan did not deny it, his mother remarked: "Well, we're going to have to tell your father."

When they got home, his father was digging postholes for a new sheep enclosure. His mother spoke to him first, without Milan present. When his mother left, Milan sat on the ground near his father and waited for him to say something.

It was another of those moments Milan will always remember. His father began quietly:

"Look, Milan, either you want to get married, or you have to get married. Which is it?"

I put a brave face on it and lied. "I want to get married."

Father replied, "And you're planning for this to last for the rest of your life?"

I wanted to wriggle out of it: "Well … I want to marry her."

Father tried again: "You know that as soon as the child is born, there's no such thing as maybe *anymore. It's a commitment for life. If you have a family and you don't look after them, it's as though you heap shit on your own head. You won't be able to smell it all the time, but every once in a while you'll get a whiff."*

It was clear to me that he was describing a sense of guilt that would stay with me as long as I lived. My parents left the decision about Růženka to me. On the way back to Bratislava I felt a thousand pounds lighter, but my conscience still weighed heavily on me. Another lesson from my parents, which, to this day, I am still absorbing.

The wedding took place in Bratislava just as Milan was finishing his army service. Milan's parents did not attend. Růženka came to stay with Milan just before the birth. The child, a boy called Milan after his father, was born in Slaný.

12

Hell's Devils

WHEN HIS MILITARY SERVICE was over, Milan announced he was definitely finished with soccer, which turned out to be somewhat premature, and he had definitely decided to leave the country. It is never easy to make complex decisions, especially when one's future is at stake, but making such decisions is always easier than carrying them out. Several years would pass before he followed through on his intentions. In the meantime, there were a couple of details to attend to. Now that he and Růženka had a child, he had to find a job. His father invited him to join his new business in Šumava, a proposition not without risks. By that time, many Communist doctrines had lost their lustre, but any kind of private enterprise was still illegal, though that certainly didn't bother Milan or his father: business was a passion for both of them, and they were willing to

Milan after his discharge from the army, 1962.

risk losing their freedom for it. After all, Milan's father had a prison record to prove it!

So the mill-less miller became a lumberjack. He set up a logging camp in Šumava and worked with his friends, felling trees and cutting them into neat logs. He invited his son to join them, but he didn't have much to offer: "You'll be working outside in the fresh air, and it'll make you healthy and strong," he said. But it wasn't that easy:

Dad was delighted to have me join him. He showed me how to cut the branches off a felled tree. He'd walk along the tree trunk and lop off an enormous limb with each swing of the axe. I tried it, braving clouds of mosquitos, but even though I was young and fit from playing sports, it took me two or three swipes of the axe to cut each limb. I decided that I wasn't cut out for this kind of work. I buried the axe in a tree and said, "Dad, I'm sorry, but this kind of work is not for me. I'm going home and I'll find something else." I expected him to blow up. But he said nothing. And before he returned from the woods in the autumn, I had found work as a repairman. This turned out to be very important, because I learned how to weld, which came in handy when I eventually escaped to the West.

Milan got the position through his brother, who at the time was working in the factory where they made prefabricated panels used in the construction of apartment buildings. Milan's job was to repair and maintain the machines they used in the production process — cement mixers, pumps, and so on.

I had no experience repairing machines, but I like to learn new things and they were willing to teach me. One of the foremen in the factory was a young lad — younger than I was — who knew members of a fairly decent rock group. For some reason, he thought I'd make a good promotions manager for them. He was something of a misfit, and he probably saw in me a similar independence of mind. He introduced me to the boys, and they agreed to let me organize a concert for them. I set up a gig in Brandýsek. In the process, I met a very capable fellow from Prague, who looked at me and said, "Why are you wasting your time with these amateurs? Come on, I'll introduce you to a really good group."

That group was called Hell's Devils, who, in terms of talent and popularity, were comparable to an officially approved group called Olympik. I could see at once how good they were, and I gave up on the local band and, from then on, devoted myself to setting up gigs for Hell's Devils.

One of the things that impressed Milan was the group's American name. He had always admired all things American, and it had already gotten him into trouble. When he was twelve, the secret police, having failed to get anywhere with his mother, tried to win over Milan. One of the cops took him to a hilltop above the pond at the cottage and told him how the Soviet Red Army had liberated the country. But Milan saw things differently. And because he was from a family of "obstinate children of God" (even though he was not religiously inclined), it was practically impossible to get him to agree to something he didn't believe in. So Milan replied that, all in all, he liked Americans better. "That made my father's time in prison even worse," he recalls. "They told my mother, 'This boy of yours is going to end up just like his father.'" Milan was impressed by the Hell's Devils' refusal to cave into the regime's demands.

Like the Plastic People of the Universe later, they resolutely sang in English; they refused to sing politically approved material; they refused to cut their hair and to cultivate a "well-groomed" image like Olympik, a group that performed in the approved manner and were meant to set an example to young working-class music lovers. Not only did Hell's Devils refuse to give themselves a Czech name, they identified stylistically with undesirable elements in the West — they wore blue jeans, played loudly, and had a repertoire of cover songs from groups like the Rolling Stones and singers like Cliff Richard. As a result, they lost their legal status and were forced to go underground. That only whetted the appetite of young people who idealized the West and drew in bigger crowds to their concerts.

I organized a gig for them in Brandýsek, a place I had already had my eye on for my earlier group. I rented a typical village hall where, for as long as anyone could remember, they had held dances where the village gentlemen spun their ladies on the dance floor to the familiar sounds of a brass band. It was a room on the second floor, with a taproom on the ground floor. It had a capacity for about a hundred people — a place like the setting for Miloš Forman's unforgettable film The Firemen's Ball.

On the day of the concert, I was very nervous. I had no idea if anyone would come. About an hour before the concert, I opened the window and looked at the highway that ran between Prague and Slaný. I saw something like a pilgrimage to a holy place: a crowd of young people were walking along the highway towards Brandýsek, and within a minute, the hall was full and crowds spilled out into the garden, the sidewalks, and the surrounding village streets. It was impossible to walk through the crowd, let alone drive through by car. We opened the windows so the music could be heard outside. The Hell's Devils did not disappoint their fans. The crowd went crazy, and when I went downstairs to the taproom for a soft drink and looked up, I could see the ceiling vibrating overhead.

I felt that all hell might break loose and the police could come any minute and arrest us all, so to be on the safe side, I took the cash box with all the money that we'd collected at the door and pushed through the crowd to my aunt's house, which was not far away. There I counted the money and made an envelope for each of the musicians. Soon my curiosity got the better of me, so I stuck the envelopes into a bag and set out for the hall. The police hadn't shown up, and so after the concert was over, I handed the money out to the boys, to their great satisfaction.

It took a while for the crowd to disperse, but no one wanted to go home. I suggested that we should go to my place at the mill, which was not far away. There was lots of room, and I knew that my parents would welcome us. Everyone agreed, so we set out — the Hell's Devils, their girlfriends, and me. I don't even remember who slept where. A picturesque pathway wound past the mill and up the hill. There was a small chapel at the top. I saw the drummer of the group, Miroslav Schwarz, who called himself "Tony Black," and his girl walking up towards the chapel. At the time, he had very long hair flowing down his back, and to this day, I remember how he and his girl walked hand in hand, their hair streaming out behind them like horses' manes. It was a very romantic moment.

I organized two more appearances for the Hell's Devils before the authorities put a stop to it. The boys had no permit. The manager of the group, Evžen Fiala, went to prison for the crime of being a subversive influence on young people, and the group had to disband. A big concert that I had planned for Okoř never happened.

The Hell's Devils playing under the portrait of Antonín Novotný, the Czechoslovak president at the time.

His time as an organizer for the Hell's Devils confirmed Milan's entrepreneurial flair. He was able to use the talents of the group to satisfy the longing of young people for the spontaneous delights of rock and roll, while at the same time making good use of his position as a member of the Communist-controlled Czechoslovak Union of Youth. The branch to which he belonged had about 250 members. He persuaded them (perhaps because he promised them 40 percent of the profits, and as the well-known Communist saying has it, "money talks") that a Hell's Devils concert — even though it was not really the kind of activity recommended or approved for "socially conscious" young people — was worthy of their sponsorship because it reflected the spirit of the times. And he was right about that. The Communist regime was already showing ideological cracks: "The period was much more relaxed, and despite resistance from the establishment, hippie culture, as it did in America, began to take root in our country as well."

First Exile

FOR MILAN, the breakup of the Hell's Devils was the last straw. His marriage to Růženka was on the rocks, and he and Milena had been planning to escape almost from the moment they first met. Milena had an uncle in Vienna who was willing to send her an invitation, and Milan — thanks to Míša — already had an invitation to Paris, so it wouldn't have been a huge problem for them simply to leave for the West legally. By now it was the mid-'60s; just a few years earlier — when people were still sneaking across the border, where they risked being attacked by savage dogs or shot by the border guards — such a scenario would have been unimaginable.

In the end, Milan decided he would go first. "I got on my motorbike and drove across the border into Germany." And just like that, he was in the West! The ease of his departure would have seemed like a fairy tale to those who escaped in the late 1940s and '50s, but by the mid-'60s, the promise of the Prague Spring could already be felt in the air, and Milan's relatively painless departure was no longer exceptional.

Milan had no intention of going to Paris. He wanted to remain in Germany. He spoke decent German, a confirmation of one of Milan's basic precepts — that you never know what might come in handy. He had decided to go alone because he didn't want to expose Milena to so much uncertainty. He was also unsure how she would react. It had not escaped his attention, even though he could not clearly articulate it at the time, that Milena had no clear notion of what she wanted for the future. "She had no desire for a career of her own," Milan says. "Or even for a family. It was as though she and her family felt above it all."

Milan's father had given him 450 American dollars, which Milan hid in the motorbike.

"A few kilometres after I crossed the border, I stopped and took a deep breath and said, 'Okay, I'm free!' A few minutes later, I was drenched in the sweat of cold reality. What was I going to do now?"

His father had given him the address of a friend — a businessman in Munich who owned a tractor motor factory where Milan might find a job as a quality controller. But he had also agreed to rendezvous with Milena in Vienna. What he hadn't realized, until his father's friend in Munich drew his attention to it, was that as soon as he crossed the border into Germany, he would be unable to leave that country for several months and thus be unable to go to Austria and help arrange for Milena's asylum there. Moreover, he felt a growing uncertainty, not only because his German was still relatively weak, but also because he'd begun to doubt his ability to make his way in an environment where he had no backup. At home, there was always a safety net of sorts. If you went for two or three weeks without work, the government would find you a job. The prospect of being jobless in the West alarmed him. How would he pay for food and accommodation? Suddenly, he was not at all certain how to proceed. He remembered his father's warning that the West was a jungle where it was every man for himself. But what weighed most heavily on his heart was the fear he might lose Milena. For although he'd known many beautiful girls before, Milena's natural beauty, a certain reserve in her character, and her inner strength convinced Milan she would make a wonderful partner in life and future mother of his children. So he decided to go back to get her.

Approaching the Czechoslovak border, he asked himself a blunt question: "What's the matter with you? You set out on a journey like this, and now you're going back without even asking what the requirements are for legal asylum!"

He stopped in a small city called Bayreuth, although Milan wasn't sure of its name at the time because his interests were far more basic than Wagner's *Ring of the Nibelung,* which was first showcased there. In Bayreuth, he looked around for an office that could provide him with information about applying for asylum, but the first place he came across was a church.

The church reminded him of an episode from his childhood. When he was in grade two, even though he was not religiously inclined, he began to serve as an altar boy for the priest in Dřetovice. A few years later, during mass, his friend, who was also an altar boy, accidentally dropped the little bell, which started rolling down the aisle, disrupting the solemn atmosphere. When the mass was over, the priest dragged his friend into the sacristy, slapped him, and berated him in language worthy of an old sea dog.

"At the time I thought that the good Lord shouldn't have had to listen to such language and see such behaviour. In the end, the Communists framed the priest, found him guilty of larceny and embezzling church funds, and sent him to prison," Milan says.

Standing in front of the church in Bayreuth, he was reminded of that incident. "A lot of people were filing into the church and I wasn't used to seeing that." (The Communist regime actively discouraged people from going to church.) "I sat in the pews at the back, and I was almost moved to tears, not only by my own fate but also by the strength of the people in the church, people that I didn't even know."

That evening, he had a lot to think about. But he was young, and the next day, after a good night's sleep, he set out for the police station. He spoke politely in German, and the police confirmed that after being granted asylum in Germany, he would not be permitted to travel abroad for three months and would, therefore, not be able to go to Vienna to meet Milena. In the middle of this friendly conversation, he found himself suddenly at a loss for words, and a minor miracle occurred, the kind that occasionally happens in Milan's life: one of the policemen said to Milan, in perfect Czech: "Say it in Czech and I'll translate it for you." All the formalities were quickly explained. The other policemen left, leaving Milan alone with the Czech-speaking German policeman, who asked him: "So what would you like to do?"

Milan outlined his plans to go back to Czechoslovakia for his fiancée and then return to Germany. "He heard me out, and then after a long pause, he asked, 'Mind if I give you some advice?' 'Of course,' I replied. 'If I were you,' said my new benefactor, 'I wouldn't stay in Germany. You can be here for fifty years and you'll still be a foreigner. There are three countries where you can feel at home as an immigrant — America, Australia, and Canada. But in my opinion, Canada is paradise.' That made an impression on me."

When he reached the border (and afterwards at work and to his friends), he explained his return by saying his motorcycle had broken

The parish church in Dřetovice, where Milan served as an altar boy.

down. Some thought he had actually tried to escape and was stupid enough to have returned. As he was approaching home in Dřetovice, he saw his mother in the distance, walking home with a bag full of groceries. He turned off his motor before she could hear it and approached her slowly. He was so afraid she might think he'd screwed up that he immediately started explaining himself. "Mum, I've just come back for a while because I needed time to catch my breath. But don't worry, I'll be leaving again soon and it'll be okay."

When his father came home, Milan kept out of sight at first. When he finally revealed himself, his father said, " So, you opened your big mouth and they sent you back."

Milan said, "That was one of the few times my father was wrong. But when I explained that I didn't feel ready yet for emigration, he understood and helped me get ready for my second attempt. But he made me give him back the 450 American dollars."

The next day, Milan travelled to Pardubice to see Milena. He told her he wasn't going anywhere without her. She was eighteen years old and in love, so those words must have sounded enormously sweet to her.

Milan didn't get his job at the Institute of Hematology back, though one can hardly blame them, since he hadn't even told them he was leaving. But he soon found work as a maintenance man in an asphalt plant in Středokluky, not far from Prague. Until December 17, he continued to live with the old lady in Ruská Street in Prague, resuming his old lifestyle of endless get-togethers and parties.

"I had lost sight of my goal, and my father had to call me out on that."

Second Exile

DECEMBER 17, 1966, came sooner than Milan had expected. The four months since his return from his first exile went by like four weeks. That day, Milan said farewell to his kindhearted old landlady, moved out of his lodging on Ruská Street, and with an air ticket from Prague to Paris in his pocket, went to spend his final night in Dřetovice. His father clearly assumed they would never see each other again. He woke Milan at five in the morning, which didn't make Milan feel very kindly towards him and Milan didn't hesitate to let him know it. His father wanted to leave Milan with a couple of final pieces of advice, including the one about the West being a jungle where "no one will really care about you." Yet that was where he was sending his son.

Naturally, he was aware that Milan's thoughts, if he had any at all at five in the morning, were elsewhere, but that didn't stop him.

"I know this advice probably won't mean very much to you now," he said, "but don't ignore it. One day, you'll understand and it will come in handy. If you ever find yourself in a situation where you don't even have enough to buy bread, always rely on yourself and concentrate on your goal. You'll see that if you stick it out, you'll eventually be okay. The main thing is never fight for someone else's interests."

Milan's father was probably thinking of the Foreign Legion, whose agents had lured quite a few young refugees into signing on, after filling their heads with false dreams of glory with a machine gun in their hands. He also reminded Milan of his metaphor of the stars: "You know there are millions of stars whirling around, each one representing an opportunity. The point of life is to learn how to catch one of these stars and not let it go. Should it ever slip out of your grasp, let it go, and don't look back; keep looking ahead and grab another one. There are many such stars, and we all have the same opportunity. But not everyone knows how to keep that single star in sight, to grasp it and hang onto it."

It was years before Milan really understood this metaphor, but he draws inspiration from it to this day. Milan's father also warned him not to tell anyone he intended to escape: "You're already on their radar, and there are a lot of secret policemen around. They are capable of stopping the aircraft and forcing you to return." And thus they said their farewells.

The plan was that his brother, Ladislav, would take him by motorbike to the nearest airport bus. Saying goodbye to his mother complicated his departure.

"My mother had packed a lot of things for me, and she stood in the doorway and cried."

That was perhaps Milan's most difficult moment; his relationship with his mother was the most powerful and constant emotional bond in his life. Whether it was his long farewell to his mother or something else, the two brothers set out from Dřetovice late and the bus left without Milan. So they chased after it. It must have been a bit like a circus act: Milan riding postilion with a suitcase in each hand. They caught up with the bus in Středokluky, and Milan boarded and found a seat beside a kid he knew from work. The boy saw that Milan had two suitcases and asked him where he was going. Milan hesitated for a moment and then admitted he was going to Paris. When the boy remarked, "Don't do a bunk on us," Milan forgot his father's warning and said, "So what if I did?" and then instantly regretted having said it.

When the bus arrived at the airport, his brother was there waiting for him. To this day Milan doesn't know why his brother didn't take him all the way to the airport. They had one last drink together, and then Milan took his suitcases to the customs checkpoint where the chief customs officer, who looked terrific in her uniform, turned out to be Marie from Dřetovice, the woman who had left an indelible mark on Milan's life by, as he gratefully remembers, "taking something that one can only lose once in a lifetime."

Their encounter at the airport went smoothly. Milan got through customs with no problems and took his seat in the Tupolev aircraft.

Not long afterwards, I heard the crescendo of powerful jet engines. I breathed a sigh of relief. My worries had been for nothing after all. However, the roar of the engines suddenly began to subside, and the stewardess announced, "We're very sorry, but we have to ask the passengers to change planes."

I suddenly felt the same sense of powerlessness I had experienced as a six-year-old boy when the secret policemen in long coats dragged my father away in that black limousine. "This is it," I thought. "Now they're going to haul me off the plane and throw me in jail." But fate was kinder to me than it had been to my father. There really was something wrong with the plane, and after another farewell drink with my brother, I was finally in the air over Europe and on my way to Paris. The plane landed at Orly.

After disembarking, I went to pick up my suitcases. I saw a long escalator in front of me and forgot about them. I had only ever seen an escalator once before in my life, in the White Swan department store in Prague, but it never actually worked. And so for the next ten minutes I rode up and down the escalators, experiencing the miracle of technology. But then I came to my senses and said to myself that it might not be a bad idea to go looking for my suitcases. To my astonishment, they were sitting there, in the middle of a concourse, crowds of people flowing around them without paying the slightest bit of attention. A porter must have picked them up and put them in a convenient place. My Czech suitcases didn't interest anyone enough to steal them.

At Orly, Milan not only realized no one was interested in stealing his Czech suitcases, but for the first time in his life, he experienced what it means to be utterly incapable of making oneself understood. Speaking in Czech was, understandably, out of the question, and the French responded with undisguised distaste at his attempts to speak German. Milan concluded that not enough time had passed since the end of the war and that the humiliation of the German occupation was still an open wound.

Paris

WHEN HE WAS IN MUNICH on his first attempt at "exile," Milan had had with him the address of a friend of his father's who had helped him out. Now, in Paris, he had an address provided by one of his mother's close friends. Milan, you might say, was born into a family with connections. This connection was the woman whom everyone in the mill in Dřetovice had called "Auntie." Her daughter had married a Frenchman who owned a bookshop in Paris, and she had emigrated with her daughter. Milan was convinced people were always willing to help each other out, so he had no hesitation about getting in touch. He got into a taxi outside the airport and showed the driver a piece of paper with the address on it. With his father's American dollars in his pocket, his self-confidence had returned. The taxi driver stopped in front of a bookstore in a picturesque little square on rue Vavin. It was a Saturday evening, just before a long weekend; the bookstore was closed and he had no other address for Auntie. As he looked around, he saw a red sign on a nearby building that said Hotel Americain.

The red sign appealed to my adventurous spirit, and so I walked over. At first, the concierge gave me an ugly look. I had started speaking to him in German, but probably from my Czech accent he realized that I wasn't German and deigned to rent me a room. In the end, business is business, and American dollars are its lingua franca. The hotel was small, and it looked comfortable enough. But even though I was just a country lad from a flour mill in Strašecí, I was shocked by the primitive conditions. The concierge led me through the building, which was built around an internal courtyard, and took me up a steep staircase into a modest little room with a small bed that was not much more luxurious than an army cot. A washbasin stood in the corner along with a water jug. There was a communal bathroom in the corridor.

But even though he had expected more of Paris and of capitalist luxury than this little hotel offered, Milan was not greatly perturbed. He knew what was important and what wasn't, and what he could change and what he could not, and at that moment, what he was really looking forward to was an evening stroll through the City of Lights. This venerable metropolis, once a tiny fishing village conquered by Julius Caesar in 52 BC, had a shining reputation that not even the Iron Curtain could conceal from him. Milan did some basic ablutions, changed his clothes, and set out to explore the city.

A few steps from the entrance to his hotel, a bevy of beautiful young women were gathered, some of them leaning nonchalantly against a wall, talking and laughing among themselves. As soon as

Milan appeared, they all smiled at him and tried to engage him in conversation, first in French and then in English, two languages that, at that time, Milan did not speak. They ignored his German, either because they didn't understand it, or because, as Milan assumed, they despised it as the language of their recent occupiers. No conversation took place. Milan's reaction was interesting: "I was quite vain at the time, and I knew that girls found me very attractive, but on the other hand, for God's sake, I'm certainly no Apollo! I walked right past them and shortly after arrived at the main boulevard, which led to the famous Champs-Elysées. I sat down in a small café, ordered a coffee, and slowly began to absorb the enormous significance of this moment in my life."

Milan knew there was no turning back, and that the way home was closed to him, if not forever (as his father had assumed), then for a long time, if only because he'd never be able to look his father in the eye if he returned. Moreover, he'd already begun to spend the American dollars his father had given him. But Milan was always one to look ahead, and also, at that moment, he was gripped by a sense of adventure and by the excitement of new beginnings. He paid for his coffee and slowly walked back to the hotel.

"When I arrived at the little square where the hotel was, a green Fiat stopped beside me. There was a pretty girl in the car, and she beckoned me inside. By this time, I'd begun to see the light and replied in German. Once again, that language saved me. The girl slammed the door in disgust and drove off in search of a more promising customer."

Milan spent the weekend wandering around the neighbourhood, and on Tuesday, he put on his best clothes again and went to visit Auntie in the bookstore. Her daughter's French husband had died, and the two of them now ran the store together. When Auntie asked him where he was staying, he pointed across the street to the neon sign that said Hotel Americain. Milan remembers clearly how the muscles in her face tightened: "Don't you know what that is? It's a hotel they rent out to prostitutes by the hour. Don't tell anyone where you live!" In any case, Milan had no one else to tell, and he had gotten used to the hotel, so he stayed there until the end of his time in Paris.

Before he left Paris, Auntie invited him to her apartment for a proper "French-style" meal. When he arrived, not only did she welcome him warmly, but she covertly pressed fifty francs into his hand. He sat down at the family table, and because he was young and famished from his wanderings through pre-Christmas Paris, he unabashedly filled his plate with a large helping of the first course, which was pickled herring. He was taken aback to see Auntie and her daughter staring at him in disbelief. When he politely refused several further courses, they asked anxiously whether he didn't like the food or he was just no longer hungry. He told them he was used to having just soup followed by a single course. They found this very amusing, though, of course, Auntie recalled this was the custom back home.

When Auntie left the room, her daughter also tried to give him fifty francs, and when Milan refused, she asked him why he didn't want to take the money. Milan told her that he couldn't reveal the reason to her. This aroused her curiosity, and she was so insistent he finally blurted out the truth. "Your mother has already given me fifty francs, but she told me not to tell anyone, and now I've broken my promise."

In the end, he accepted and then went to Auntie to explain to her what had happened. He didn't want to appear to be a moocher.

The two women also gave Milan metro tickets, which he used to explore Paris. He would take the subway, travel a random number of stops, get off, and look around.

One day I came out of the metro and suddenly there before me was the most famous symbol of Paris — the Eiffel Tower. I think it made such a profound impression on me because I hadn't gone looking for it. I hadn't set out to find it. I discovered it the way Columbus discovered America.

When I think back on that moment, I realize that I have a similar approach to business. That is one of the keys to my success, and may also be the reason I'm not only still enjoying success in my seventies but am still excited by it. Some people buy maps and set off for a specific destination. I enjoy discovering things by chance and letting them have an impact on me, offer me possibilities. It could be a new technique for cleaning the commercial spaces in a supermarket more efficiently and more economically than my competition, or constructing a new runway at the airport, or discovering a quality in my employees that suggests a way of giving them new opportunities to excel.

Whatever it is, I think I've retained an ability to live life without prejudging things. That doesn't mean I don't start out with a particular idea. But every idea has to have a certain openness and flexibility to it. If all we see is the plan we've laid down for ourselves, we lose the ability to respond to the unexpected. If we are inflexible, any stumbling block can lead to disappointment and discouragement. Even if an idea completely blows up on me, I always try to take something positive from what's left, find a couple of pebbles with which I can go on building, perhaps making something far better than what I'd originally imagined. Just think, if ten boys had been given tickets to the Paris metro, each one would have used his tickets differently. I don't say that my way is better, but the way I used those tickets at the time is a measure of how I'm different from the others. Each of us is different, and we each have opportunities in life. For me, at the time, those tickets were one of those little stars, one tiny opportunity, though I hadn't really understood it that way at the time.

Even now, Milan has an aversion to conventional systems for running a business. It bothers him that everything has to be done according to a business plan. He lets his employees work out a plan for themselves, and then he vets it, but he's never a slave to it. He looks for the potential in it. Otherwise, he says, he would "die of boredom."

From the Eiffel Tower, he went home by taxi, and as he was paying the driver, an incident occurred that says a lot about Milan's personality. He thanked the driver in German and then tipped him the change. Because he hadn't yet mastered French money, he had no idea how much the coins he had given the driver were worth. The driver took one look at them and tossed them over his shoulder, where they rolled around on the seat and onto the floor. It was his way of protesting about the insultingly small amount Milan had given him. Milan picked up some of the coins and flung them back at the driver. At the same time, a conviction that would become one of the hallmarks of his attitude to life flashed through his mind: "I may be a refugee, but no one is ever going to humiliate me like that again!"

Later, when he was hiring new employees, he always treated immigrants with respect, regardless of how poor their English was.

A few days later, just before Christmas, Auntie's daughter took him to the train station.

16

In the Refugee Camps

AT THE STATION, Milan bought a train ticket to Vienna, where he had arranged to meet Milena. The train he boarded in Paris was going to Prague, so he asked a young German woman who was sitting opposite him to be sure to wake him up at Nuremberg, where he was to change trains for Vienna. The last thing he wanted was to end up back in Prague, possibly to spend Christmas in prison.

Instead, he spent it in Vienna. On Christmas Day, he went to a small café owned by Milena's uncle, who was originally a Sudeten German from Moravia, close to the Austrian border, an area from which Sudeten Germans had been expelled after the war. Milena's uncle had married an Austrian woman, but he welcomed Milan in perfect Czech. Despite his unceremonious deportation from Czecho-slovakia, he appeared to hold no grudge against the Czechs.

The border checkpoint near Salzburg, where Milan and Milena made their illegal crossing into Germany, 1967.

Milena had planned a two-week visit with her uncle in Vienna immediately after Christmas, though neither her parents nor her uncle knew of her intention to emigrate. She had arranged to go by train to Vienna with a married couple, Karel and Milena Brejcha, who were also planning to escape, but that plan fell through. In the end, she was driven to Vienna by a business associate of her father's, a Mr. Florian and his wife, who had been expelled by the Communists and settled in Vienna. On the appointed day Milan, unaware of their last-minute change of plans, went to the train station to meet Milena and got a shock when only the Brejchas showed up. They explained Milena would be arriving later, as planned, by car. He went to wait for her in front of her uncle's café, but when it got late and she still hadn't shown up, he went back to his hotel. Milena arrived later that night, and Milan met her the following day.

That small glitch may have saved Milena's attempt to escape, because if Milena and the Florians had met Milan at the uncle's café, Mr. Florian might have realized that Milena was attempting to make a run for it, and might well have made her get back in the car, taken her across the Czechoslovak border to Bratislava, a short drive away, and put her on an express train back to Prague. But that didn't happen, and Milena concluded thankfully that the god of lovers must have been on their side. The only problem was, because they hadn't revealed their plans to Milena's parents, her family reported her missing to Interpol when she failed to return after two weeks. In the end, Milena wrote them a heartfelt letter of apology to smooth things over.

When the lovers and the Brejchas met the following day, they bought train tickets to Salzburg, close to the German border. Milan was the only one who had the papers to enter Germany, so in Salzburg, they got off the train and went to the German consulate to get

permission to enter the country. They were refused, so they decided
to cross the border illegally. They took their suitcases and began walking along the autobahn. It was a complicated situation, but it could
have been far more difficult had Růženka allowed their son, Milan Jr.,
who was now four, to go with them, as Milena had suggested.

Milena remembers this memorable trek, which happened on
New Year's Eve: "To this day, I can still feel the mud and the snow and
the many runs in my devastated stockings, which were only partially
covered by a miniskirt and leather boots."

As they were walking along, a police van pulled up and two border guards jumped out and demanded to see their papers. Milan, whose documents were in order, was allowed to continue, but the others were told they had to go back. Milan cranked up his eloquence, and it may have helped, because one of the border guards said to the other: "Let them be. They'll be arrested at the border anyway." They drove off, and Milan — not feeling entirely confident — set off on his own to deal with the German border guards. The guards looked through the documents while Milan told them his story. They must have been impressed, because one of them said to Milan, "If you can bring them here, we'll make sure that you all get to Nuremberg."

The German authorities were waiting for them on the other side of the border. They took a bus to a refugee centre located in old military barracks in Nuremberg. In a large hall that had probably been a gymnasium, their identities were confirmed and they were then sent to their quarters, the men to the men's barracks, which had about twenty beds in it, and Milena and Milena Brejcha to the women's barracks. They were free to come and go as they liked during the day, though they had the feeling they were being watched. Most of the refugees in the camp were from Czechoslovakia, but there were also some from other countries, especially Hungary and Yugoslavia. Most of the Czechs and Slovaks stuck together, though a handful of nationalistic Slovaks, who claimed Slovakia was a separate country, formed their own little group.

One evening, Milan overheard an interesting conversation in the bunk below him between two young Czechs that reminded him of his father's warning. One of them said to the other: "Look, just remember one thing. Don't ever sign up for the French Foreign Legion."

It was as though Milan was hearing the voice of his own father warning him never to fight for foreign interests:

It gave me goose bumps to hear that kid's story about escaping from the French Foreign Legion. His regiment had been sent to Addis Ababa, the capital of Ethiopia. Discipline was very strict, and the boy had done something that landed him in the brig. That happened in other armies as well, but in Addis Ababa they had especially drastic re-education techniques. The prisoners were given rucksacks that had electrical cords instead of shoulder straps. They had to fill their rucksacks with stones and, shirtless, were forced to carry the stones from one pile to another in the burning African sun. Under the weight of the rucksack, the electrical cords cut into the flesh of their shoulders, where the blood mixed with the salt in their perspiration. When they had transferred all the stones, they were ordered to carry them back to their original location. The punishment wasn't just physical; it also wore them down psychologically. When the young Czech legionnaire reached the end of his tether, he went AWOL. *During the day, he buried himself in the sand to hide from the helicopters that were looking for deserters. At night, he fled on foot or hid himself among the cargo on transport trucks. Finally, he managed to catch a boat back to Europe. He was lucky, because deserters were being shot. Was that story a message from my father? In any case, I didn't sleep much that night.*

The next day, after having breakfast together in the large mess hall, the two couples were summoned to an interview. The officials explained that refugees had to submit a request for asylum in the country where they crossed the Czechoslovak border, which meant Milan was the only one who could stay in Germany; the others would have to return to Austria. Milan tried unsuccessfully to persuade the German official to let the whole group stay in Germany, so in the end, they decided to go back together.

Using money the Germans had given them, the group took a train from Nuremberg to Salzburg and presented themselves to the police. From then on, a policeman accompanied Milan everywhere, even to the bathroom. Milan and the others went through the same disillusionment as millions of other refugees who, at certain points in their exile, felt they had sacrificed everything to reach freedom in the West, only to be treated like criminals, or at the very least like outcasts.

That same evening, along with two other refugees, they were loaded into a police van and driven to an unknown destination. Milan thought they were taking them to a hotel, and when, in answer to his question the guard answered, "To jail!" he thought it was a joke. When he translated the "joke" to the others, they all burst out laughing. "You'll soon be laughing on the other side of your face!" the policeman said.

Just before midnight, the police van stopped in front of a high wall. Milan felt unusually anxious, mainly because of Milena, for whom he felt responsible. Once inside, he paid close attention to his fellow detainees during the hour-long walks in the prison courtyard. He talked to some of the prisoners, including a thief and even a murderer, but no one could explain why they were there.

Eventually, he found out what he needed to know by prying information out of one of the guards. Evidently, the police were waiting until sufficient numbers of refugees had arrived to make it worthwhile to transport them all at once to Traiskirchen refugee camp in Vienna. That lifted Milan's spirits a little. They were keeping them in custody so that they wouldn't wander about the city. He was also upset by a physical examination that required him to strip in front of a doctor. Milan knew it was only a security measure to prevent the spread of infectious diseases, but he felt it was also the Austrians' way of expressing their superiority over the refugees. Removing his Jockey shorts was doubly difficult for him at the time, because apart from his natural modesty, he had the remaining American dollars his father had given him sewn into his underwear. He held the underwear close to his body and clung to it like a leech. The doctor, who clearly thought Milan was shy, laughed and told him to get dressed.

Life with Bedbugs

T**HE FORCES AND PASSIONS** that shaped the second half of the twentieth century, as well as the genes and circumstances that formed the lives of the characters in this story, are the stuff of great drama. Of the two grand ideologies that dominated the last century, neither the Nazi madness that proclaimed a thousand-year Reich nor the insanity of the Soviet Union's intention to dominate Central and Eastern Europe "for all time" was able to prevail in the end. The demise of the Communist dictatorship, when it finally arrived, was less horrific than the crushing of Nazi Germany and Hitler's suicide in the Berlin bunker, but in 1966, when Milan and Milena finally left Czechoslovakia, no one could have predicted with any certainty that Communism would ever collapse, even though the ice was already shifting. A long-ing for freedom was in the air, and in Czechoslovakia, the Prague Spring of 1968 and the hope of change it brought were not far off.

Milena and Milan brought different legacies into their life together. Milan's mother was a proud patrician with an interest in mysticism. His father was exceptionally strong and talented, a diamond in the rough from working-class origins, a tough and indomitable master of his own destiny. Time and again, he would fling his entrepreneurial glove in the face of the all-powerful regime, but to little avail. Sadly, despite enduring long years in the worst state prisons, he did not live to see the collapse of the regime. He did, however, live to see the beginnings of his son's entrepreneurial success.

Milena's father was similar to Milan's. He was an excellent chemist who tried his hand at business even after the Communist takeover, though he didn't get very far: he was arrested on the same day his wife had a gallbladder operation and he then spent five years in prison. Understandably, there was no love lost between him and the Communists. Like a large part of the population, however, he eventually came to terms with them, because it appeared they would be in power forever. Milena's maternal grandfather was a successful lawyer and a prominent member of the Communist Party. His influence extended all the way to Bratislava where, within two weeks, he was able to arrange Milan's divorce from Růženka.

But he wasn't thrilled with the idea of having Milan as a grand-son-in-law, and when he learned of it, he was certainly not thrilled by Milena's escape to the West. So one small drama in the biggest ideological conflict of the twentieth century was playing out at the very heart of the founding families of this new dynasty. I don't think one could claim the "ideology of freedom" triumphed in this case; the real victor was the eternal, and sometimes fickle, sorceress, Love.

Milena had told no one except Milena and Karel Brejcha of her plan to flee to the West with Milan. Her family had assumed that once she had graduated from the sugar processing industrial school and found a job in her field, she would forget about him. For them, Milan was just a country boy and, worse, an adventurer and a dreamer who would never amount to anything. Later, they resented Milan's father for encouraging his son to escape, and they also believed he must have known of Milena's intention to run away with Milan.

In fact, Milan's father did know about Milena's intentions, but he didn't know she hadn't told her parents, or even the Florians, who took her across the border. Yet it was the Florians, in particular Mr. Florian, who eventually played a big role in reconciling both families. Initially, Mr. Florian had been very critical of Milan, but he grew to respect him. He was impressed by how hard Milan worked, not only on weekdays in the Betonwerke, a cement factory where he found temporary employment, but also on Saturdays and sometimes on Sundays, when farmers would come to the gate of Traiskirchen and select cheap labour to work in their fields and vineyards.

Mr. Florian turned out to be a particularly valuable ally during a visit from Milena's paternal grandmother. At that time, Milena was already four months pregnant and visibly so. The couple were given small private quarters in the camp. Milena decided to postpone the wedding until after the child was born, because she didn't want to appear pregnant in her wedding photos. In anticipation of the grandmother's visit, Milan and Milena spruced up their little flat so that the grandmother would be suitably impressed:

We were pretty successful, except for the bedbugs that had taken up residence in the ceiling and bombarded us every night. I went to the gate to meet Granny Bejrová and smiled pleasantly at her. For her part, she had decided not to engage with me. She had already been persuaded that I was a ne'er-do-well, unworthy of her granddaughter, and she made no effort to hide it. That was fine with me: at least we knew where we stood. The grandmother entered the room, took one look at Milena's pregnant figure, and said, "That's it, Milena. Pack your things, we're going home."

Milena stood her ground and said, "Granny, I'm sorry, but I'm staying here with Milan." The grandmother looked around angrily, and I attempted to lighten the atmosphere by inviting her to sit down. The grandmother, without thinking, snapped, "I would if there were anywhere to sit."

The grandmother stayed in Vienna for two weeks. On one occasion, Mr. Florian drove her to the camp for a visit, and on the way she carried on about what a scoundrel Milan was, predicting things would turn out badly. Mr. Florian stopped the car, turned to the grandmother, and very politely said: "Ma'am, I'm telling you, you have no idea what he's like. If you don't stop running him down right now, you can get out of the car and walk the rest of the way on your own."

"From that moment on," Milan recalls gratefully, "Granny Bejrová softened up. I don't know whether she'd really begun to appreciate my qualities or had simply given up, but from then on, she behaved quite decently towards me."

Milena's grandmother wasn't the only problem the couple faced. Milan and Milena had applied to emigrate to Canada, but when they went for their final interview with Canadian officials, they were told they couldn't travel together. Milan could go, but Milena would have to wait for three months after the baby was born so that the child's health could be vetted by a doctor.

Then there was the difference in their natures. "Milena was much more serious than I was," Milan says. "During parties with the Czechs who were also planning to go to Canada, I loved to make jokes at my own expense. Once, on the way home from a party, Milena lit into me. 'You're always playing the fool! I can't stand it!'

"When she was in her eighth month, she gave serious thought to returning home. The fact that she was alone much of the time didn't help either. I was working six, sometimes seven days a week," Milan says.

I didn't realize how much she needed my support. Not only was Milena alone, she was also suffering from hormonal changes and anxiety. Today, fathers are usually present at that miraculous moment when a child arrives in the world and their wife or partner becomes a mother. It's a crucial moment, when the family comes together as one. It was different back then: when Milena's contractions began, I was at work. They took her by ambulance to Baden bei Wien, and the first to appear at her bedside was Mr. Florian. Even though he picked me up at work and drove me to the hospital, Milena and I never had a chance to exchange tender looks or caresses. When I finally saw our son Robert, I said to myself, "What an ugly little thing!" I've always felt awkward around newborn babies.

But I soon got used to my new role as a father and began to feel a sense of responsibility for this growing little bundle who demanded so much care and attention. When Milena brought Robert home from the hospital, I'd prepared a cot with a curtain over it to protect him from the bedbugs.

It's no exaggeration to say these highly annoying insects were witnesses to the most intimate moments of this key period in Milan and Milena's life. The bond between them must have been so firm, and their dissatisfaction with their native land so deeply rooted — and, in Milan's case, the longing to fulfill the dream inspired by *In the Glow of Millions* so fundamental — that a plague of bedbugs could not discourage them. They did not give up and return home. They did not return even when, at one point, Milena sat on the edge of the bed, looked around, and burst into tears. She had put a brave face on things for so long, and now her circumstances had finally overwhelmed her. She missed her mother and her sister, and when she needed them most, here she was, sitting helplessly in a bleak refugee camp, crying her eyes out.

Milan felt strong and consoled her. "Don't worry!" he said. "I'll help you."

"Even though I refused to change the dirty diapers, which made me feel physically ill, I helped her boil them and wring them out. I could see how hard that was on Milena's hands. And because this was her first baby, Milena didn't have enough milk, so I warmed the bottles, cooked baby food, and helped feed him. I also bathed him in a small washbasin lined with diapers. All this brought our family closer together. The worst thing, though, was the bedbugs which, in spite of all the precautions we took, bothered the baby. Very often his crying would wake us up at night."

Milena and Milan on their wedding day, 1968.

Milena, baby Robert, and Milan in Vienna, February 1968.

Their final weeks in the refugee camp in Vienna were somewhat unsettled. They'd had to postpone the wedding and, with it, their departure, since they couldn't leave for Canada until little Robert was three months old.

They were married in February 1968, when Robert was two months old and the political ferment of the Prague Spring was off to an uncertain start. Milena's Uncle Hans, who had financially supported her since her arrival in Vienna, organized and paid for the wedding celebration in his café. Milan tried to refuse out of pride, but Mr. Florian brought him to his senses.

The wedding took place in a church. Even in such muddled circumstances as theirs, they still had to sort out the question of what colour the bride's dress should be. It seems the groom preferred white, and the bride was against it, because, as she said, "I already have a child, and you've already been to the altar once before."

"I have not," Milan objected. "My first wedding was a civil ceremony."

 Milan and Milena have pleasant memories of the event. "Milena looked very lovely in a simple knee-length dress. Even though neither of us was religious, the wedding in the church was beautiful. There were about fifty guests, and Uncle Hans invited them all to dinner. Karel and Milena Brejcha were our witnesses. Little Robert slept through the ceremony in a basket on one of the pews and never cried once. There was no honeymoon. After dinner, we went back to the camp, gave the baby a bath, and spent our first night as husband and wife more or less the way we'd done many times before."

The Refugee Chooses a Homeland

ALTHOUGH THEY HAD MADE the decision to go to Canada together, Milena saw it as a very pragmatic decision. "There was no longing for adventure and seeing other countries in my decision," Milena says. "I felt no need to 'discover America.' I took it as part of life: I knew I'd have to adapt and find work wherever we went, and I thought it would be the same in Canada. I wasn't drawn by the romance of distant vistas, but I wasn't afraid of them either. I had already reconciled myself to the fact that I would probably never see my parents and my sister again, and I gave no thought to the possibility that I might miss European culture."

Milan's choice of a new homeland was more complicated. He and Milena hadn't brooded over their decision. "I don't remember that we had ever sat down and articulated our dreams about our future," Milan says.

At that time, my dreams were vague but teeming with possibilities. For me, Canada was a mysterious land full of secrets waiting to be uncovered. I saw the difference between Canada and the United States mainly in Canada's absolute superiority in hockey. As a twelve-year-old boy growing up in the Kladno region, two Canadian teams that came to play in Czechoslovakia made an indelible impression on me — the Whitby Dunlops and the Belleville McFarlands. The entire Whitby team, including the trainers and managers, wore coats with colourful stripes on them. They may have been the colours of the traditional Hudson's Bay blankets, but from the moment they stepped onto the ice, they made a tremendous impression and began a new fashion trend in Bohemia.

In those days, Milan was unaware the Hudson's Bay Company was founded by a Czech prince, son of the Protestant "winter" king, Frederick, and Elizabeth, daughter of the English king James I. During the English Civil War, Prince Rupert had fought on the side of his uncle, James II. After the Restoration, in 1670, his cousin Charles II signed a royal charter granting Prince Rupert, and seventeen others, a monopoly on trade in the area that drains into Hudson's Bay. This represented a gift of more than 3.9 million square kilometres, or more than a third of what now comprises Canada. The Czech connection continued into the first decade of the twenty-first century, when another refugee from the same part of Bohemia as Prince Rupert and Milan Kroupa, George Jason Heller, became president of the Hudson's Bay Company. He had come to Canada with his parents after the Communist putsch in February 1948.

But Milan's immediate reasons for deciding to emigrate to Canada had more to do with hockey:

There was also a player for the Belleville McFarlands called Al Dewsbury. We called him "Juiceberry." He wore his hair in a brush cut, and from then on, every young boy in the country wanted a haircut like it. We called it "a Canadian lawn." That was before the Beatles came along and changed the fashion again. When I was a young boy in the 1950s, my mother and I would listen to the radio broadcasts of the matches between Czechoslovakia and Canada. My mother wondered why I was so upset.

"But, Mum, it's not fair!" I said. "It's always *winter in Canada! And they can play all year round!"*

Such were the kind of romantic notions I emigrated with. They were very different from my wife's dreams.

When it came down to deciding on which of the three countries I'd dreamed about — Australia, the United States, and Canada — I rejected Australia because they were accepting Communists; I rejected the United States because I would probably have had to serve in the army and go to Vietnam, and I remembered my father's advice about not serving foreign interests. I didn't see the war in Vietnam as a struggle to liberate humanity from Communism but rather as a struggle to protect American interests. I knew that Canada was the only country in the world where people of all nationalities were somehow managing to live together. That really attracted me.

My later experience confirmed that original impression. Even though I had come from Czechoslovakia with certain prejudices about people we were used to looking down on, my first experiences in Canada were very instructive. When I went to the immigration office, they made no distinctions between us. Turkish, Chinese, Czech — they treated us all equally. I know that's not always the reality, but at the time, I was very much aware of it. I was somehow able to overlook the problem of racism. Here, I felt we all had the same opportunity. In Austria, they treated refugees differently than they treated their own citizens, and I felt that our opportunities there would be limited. Canada was the promised land for me. It has never disappointed me. It's the woman to whom I have always been faithful.

First Impressions

"**I**N THE EARLY EVENING, on March 25, 1968, in light snowfall, we landed in Montreal."

Thus, in a single sentence, does Milan describe his arrival in the promised land. They were meant to stay in Montreal, but because they had friends from the refugee camp who had emigrated to Canada several months before and settled in Toronto, the immigration official allowed them to go there as well. They spent one night in Montreal and the next morning boarded the train for Toronto, carrying three-month-old Robert in a basket between them. "I looked out the window at the enormous cars," said Milan. "To our European eyes, they seemed overwhelming. Back home, we called them 'Americas,' and now here they were, sailing by us like ships on the ocean. I wondered if I would ever end up driving something like that."

Corner of Spadina Avenue and Dundas Street West, Toronto, in the spring of 1968.

CITY OF TORONTO ARCHIVES, FONDS 1567, SERIES 648, FILE 246, ITEM 1

Milena and Milan, with Robert in the baby carrier, at the airport in Vienna, before their departure to Canada.

Their friends from the Austrian camp, a married couple called the Hlozáneks, were waiting for them at Union Station in Toronto and took them to the Hotel Astoria on the corner of Jarvis and Wellesley. Their stay was paid for by the Canadian government. The next morning, Jirka Hlozánek brought them a very practical gift: Toronto public transit tickets. Milan immediately took the bus to the immigration office. He knew he had to get out at Dundas Street. He saw the street in time, stood by the exit doors, and waited for the driver to open them. The driver apparently ignored him, because the doors remained closed. Milan pushed them. The doors still remained closed. Then he noticed the passengers were trying to explain that he should step down so that the weight of his body would automatically open the doors. At that moment, Milan's pride kicked in.

> *I understood neither what they were saying nor their gestures, and I blushed to the roots of my hair. I felt like an idiot who couldn't figure out how to get off a bus. I was so embarrassed I just wanted to disappear. So I turned around and sat down again, hoping that, at the next bus stop, someone else would leave and I could simply follow him out and then walk back one stop. Just then the driver noticed my plight and opened the doors for me. I flew out the doors and ducked behind the bus so people couldn't see me. I'd never experienced anything quite so humiliating, not since my Czech teacher in high school slapped me in front of the class.*

Milena's first impressions of Canada were shocking:

> *After the plane landed in Montreal in the snow, late in the evening, they drove us from the airport to the hotel. Milan slept on the couch, and little Robert and I slept on the bed. They woke us up early in the morning and took us to the station, where we were given train tickets to Toronto.*

I've kept that ticket to this day. At the station, we bought ourselves breakfast. I was proud to be able to use the only English expression I knew — hemendex *— in other words, "ham and eggs"! On the train trip, I began to look around. For mile after mile, the countryside never seemed to change. To my tired and sleep-deprived brain, everything appeared monotonous and forbidding. Over the same distance in Europe, we would have passed by mountains and valleys, meadows and villages, and through picturesque little towns. Desperately, I looked for something pleasant. Finally, we reached the suburbs of Toronto. Maybe here, I thought, in the second-largest city in Canada, it would be more welcoming.*

But my first impression was terrible there too. We passed by the bleak backyards of the little houses in Scarborough, then the buildings slowly got bigger and higher. In 1968, Toronto had none of the French charm and cosmopolitan self-confidence of Montreal, nor did it have the imposing skyscrapers of New York. It was more like a frumpy woman who had stopped caring about her appearance. We were lucky enough to have a few acquaintances in Toronto, like the Hlozáneks, who tried their best to make things pleasant for us. The evening we arrived, they took us for an evening drive along the Gardiner Expressway, with Lake Ontario on one side and the skyline of Toronto on the other. The most imposing building was the Royal York Hotel. But not even the vast waters of the lake, which seemed more like an inland sea, nor the lights of the big city, nor the endless streams of large American cars on the highway — none of that impressed me. In fact, I found it all shocking, but I was too tired to care.

The Hotel Astoria was anything but luxurious. They had to bathe little Robert in a very modest bathroom sink. They could not, however, stay in the hotel for long and immediately set out to look for more permanent accommodation. They drove around the city with Jirka Hlozánek, finally focussing their search on Parkdale, where many Slav immigrants, particularly Poles, lived and where to this day you can buy Polish sausages, smoked pork knuckles, pickled herring, and decent rye bread. In Parkdale, they found a cheap furnished flat on the second floor of a house owned by Yugoslavians. The Canadian government would cover the rent.

It was an unforgettable moment: "We had moved into our first family nest in a very celebratory mood," Milan recalls. "After bathing Robert, Milena and I sat on the couch and turned on the television set. We didn't understand a single word, but it gave us a feeling of domestic comfort. Suddenly, I began to feel itchy. At first, I paid no attention, but after a while, we were both squirming around because it was impossible to sit still. We jumped up from the couch. Milena pulled off the cushions to reveal a scattering herd of bedbugs!"

Milan Looks for a Star

MILAN'S FAMILY STAYED only one night in the flat they shared with the bedbugs. The next morning, they found accommodation with a Polish family on nearby Fern Street, and Milan began a course in English at a secondary school near Castle Frank, on Bloor Street, by the Don Valley. The lessons began at 3 PM, after the regular students were finished for the day. He enjoyed the cups of hot chocolate they were served during their breaks, which tasted so completely different from hot chocolate in Europe. Through the school's tall glass windows, he could see the Don Valley Parkway and the thousands of cars snaking slowly along it, and he thought of all the accidents there must have been to make the traffic move so slowly. Some people in his group were from Eastern Europe, but most of them were Chinese and Italian. In school, they were all on an equal footing, and the lingua

FACING

Milena and Robert with their first car, 1968.

franca among them was English, which hastened Milan's progress. At home, he spoke to his landlord in a mixture of Czech and Polish, but he did not feel at all like a perpetual foreigner as he had in Austria.

That period is still very vivid in his mind: "It wasn't just the absence of guards, who had kept a close eye on us in the Austrian refugee camp. I instinctively felt that this was it; we were going to be here for good. I really believed I would never go home, or see my parents, again. I took strength from the thought that I was following my father's dream."

Milan's approach to studying English was typical: "My ambition was to learn English without an accent, so no one would know I was an immigrant. It was mostly a matter of pride, but I was also influenced by my experience in the Austrian camp." His decision to make English a priority led to a break with Jirka Hlozánek. Jirka worked for a company that made metal railings, and he had arranged a job interview for Milan with his boss, who was Yugoslavian, telling him Milan was a skilled welder. This took Milan by surprise. "Jirka, I'm sorry, but I'm going to school now. I consider that more important than work at the moment."

That reply indicated not only Milan's ambition to learn English well, but also that he had not forgotten his father's advice about catching the star of opportunity and clinging to it. At that moment, the brightest star was English. He understood that Jirka might see his refusal of help as ingratitude, but his experience in Austria had taught him the enormous advantages of mastering a language, and he stuck to his decision.

Milena, however, refused to go to English classes. She expected Milan would review everything he'd learned in class with her, thus allowing her to learn English at home. She also hoped it would bring them closer together.

Milan refused to go along with this idea. "Milena was upset, but there was another problem here. I didn't always understand everything that we studied in class. When you're learning something new, you can't teach the material at the same time. I was too proud to admit my short-comings to her, and so I made all kinds of excuses instead. That made Milena mad with me. 'If you don't want to teach me,' she said, 'then I'm not going to go to school at all.' It took her five years to learn decent English."

Toronto already had a thriving Czechoslovak community. "Both of us made connections with the local Czech Sokol gymnastic club," Milena remembers. "I went there to work out, and Milan played soccer with a group of Czechs on the Sparta Toronto team, until that famous night when he came home at 3 AM with a friend, and I gave him a couple of slaps in the face in the doorway. It wasn't that he was drunk, but I'd waited up for him the whole night and was worried that something had happened to him."

Milan recalls the incident slightly differently. He remembers only one slap, which according to him, happened around eleven in the evening, not in the early hours of the morning. He'd played soccer with the Czechs on the Sparta Toronto team, whose main sponsor was Ladislav (Laddie) Myslivec, who had come to Canada in 1939 and nine years later incorporated a very successful company called Aircraft Appliances and Equipment Limited. Laddie was cut from the same cloth as Milan and was remembered in an obituary written by fellow countryman George Gross, who recalled Laddie's avid sportsmanship in soccer, volleyball, golf, and tennis, and his support of many Toronto-area sports clubs. "He enriched the life of practically everyone he came in contact with," Gross wrote in the *Toronto Telegram*. "Many tears were shed in business and sports circles, as well as among Czechs and Slovaks on both sides of the Atlantic. Yesterday even the heavens wept."

While Milan was going to school in Toronto, the Prague Spring was taking place in Czechoslovakia. His classmates would bring newspapers and articles about events there to the school, and for a while, it seemed a miracle might happen and freedom would return to their homeland. That illusion was quickly crushed by the invasion of the Warsaw Pact armies, mostly Soviet troops, on August 21, 1968. The invasion made headlines in all the newspapers: "Czechoslovakia Occupied by Warsaw Pact Armies." Milan hadn't planned on returning, but the invasion confirmed his belief that Canada would be his home until the end of his days. For the first six months, the Canadian government paid their rent and the cost of English language instruction for Milan; they also received an allowance for baby Robert and for food, clothing, and transportation. After five months of studying English, Milan began looking for work, determined to get off government support as soon as he could. (He was never a fan of government subsidies.) He found a job as a lathe operator in a factory that manufactured plastic parts in Mississauga, a suburb of Toronto. It was a long commute by public transport from their flat, but they found a used car — a Volkswagen, their first — for $500. The floor of the car was rusted through in places, so Milan could see the road below him go by as he was driving. But the feeling of confidence and independence having a car of his own gave him made up for the vehicle's shortcomings.

He passed his driver's test with flying colours. One morning, as he was driving to work, he calculated how much he was making and how much the family expenses were, and he was shocked to discover his pay was less than the support they were receiving from the government. It appeared refugees were a losing proposition for Canada. He went to his English teacher for clarification: "How can the government afford to give so much support to every immigrant? They must be going bankrupt."

The teacher laughed, patted Milan on the shoulder, and said: "They see it as an investment. Don't worry. You'll pay it back."

Milan never forgot his teacher's answer: "I think of him when I do my taxes every spring. After forty years, I've certainly paid back their investment many times over, and I'm not done yet."

To make up for the loss of income when the government grants stopped, Milena found work in Laddie Myslivec's Aircraft Appliances factory. With her new job, their family life changed again. "We began to live the frantic life of many modern Canadian families," Milan says.

We got up early, dressed the boy, who wasn't even a year old yet, and took him to a Czech woman who looked after him. Then I drove Milena to work and afterwards drove to work myself. In the evening, the merry-go-round simply reversed direction.

I was so out of sorts from this daily rat race that I felt I was beginning to lose it. One day, at breakfast, Milena was nattering on about something, and I asked her to stop because she was getting on my nerves. But she kept on talking, and I yelled at her quite crudely to shut her mouth. She kept nattering on, so I slapped her. I'd never done such a thing before, and I was shocked at my own behaviour. I'd been brought up to believe that women should not be treated that way. Feeling miserable, I shoved my plate aside and walked around the flat. Then I sat down on the bed. I had no idea what to do. How would I ever resolve this? I wasn't the type to buy flowers. As usual, Milena solved the dilemma for me without hesitation. She walked across the room, stood in front of me, and said: "So, you think you can slap me around?" Before I could reply, she slapped me once on each cheek. I began to laugh uncontrollably. "You have no idea what a help this is! I didn't know how to make it up to you, and you found a way." I was also saved the expense of a bouquet, which we could hardly have afforded.

Even with Milena's income, the family could not afford the $400 a month it would take to rent the kind of apartment they wanted. It was becoming more and more obvious to Milan that even if he and Milena worked as hard as they could, they would only be able to make enough to cover their basic needs. Milan expected more of himself: "I hadn't emigrated just to get by!" he says. "So, in the evenings, I began to comb the want ads in the papers. My attention was caught by a magical little headline that said: 'Be Your Own Boss!' It sounded like a wonderful idea."

The ad had been placed by an office-cleaning firm, and Milan went to see them the very next morning:

They immediately invited me for an interview. They started by saying how wonderful it was that, so soon after arriving in Canada, I was trying to become independent, and that success was within reach. Naturally, they said, I had to invest something, but they promised to teach me the ropes and that the investment would soon pay for itself. That was music to my ears. I agreed on the spot to pay a deposit for the use of the cleaning machines and the purchase of several cleaning contracts.

My first contract was with Beaver Air Conditioning at the intersection of the Gardiner Expressway and Kipling. I drove there with Milena and two friends, eagerly expecting that this would be our "grand opportunity." In a way it was, but I soon discovered that the people who sold me the contract saw me more as an easily exploitable sucker, rather than as a serious entrepreneur to whom they were showing the ropes. According to the law of the jungle in Western capitalism — at least as my father saw it — they were the beasts of prey and we were part of an ignorant herd. But I felt there was more at stake here than a simple job, and so I set about learning how to clean floors, take out the garbage, and do the dusting, as though it were the most honourable employment in the world.

Milena went with Milan to do the cleaning at night. Early one morning, they got back from work to find little Robert missing. They immediately feared the worst: someone had kidnapped him, or he'd somehow gotten out of the house and been run over by a car. It didn't occur to them he might simply have woken up and gone looking for his parents.

Frantically, they went searching for him. In the end, a neighbour who had seen him toddling along the street brought him home. They resolved this would never happen again. (At the time, the laws concerning parenting were not as strict as they are today, and no one turned them in.) Milena never again left little Robert at home alone.

Milan's first car in front of his first contract, 1968.

Milan took over the office cleaning himself:

As it is for so many new immigrants, my life became one round of work. In the morning, I fulfilled my usual obligations; during the day, I worked as a lathe operator; and in the evening, I picked Robert up at the nursery and Milena at Aircraft Appliances, and then drove them home. After supper, I had a brief rest, then at seven, I started cleaning. I would usually finish about three, sometimes four in the morning. It was exhausting, with no time for rest or relaxation. To this day, I have no idea how Milena and I managed. But I made an important discovery: I really enjoyed cleaning.

The rhythm of my body, the whirring of the machines, the smell of cleaning materials, and the opportunity to do something in my own way and to daydream without interruption — I enjoyed all of it. It was very different from my other daily routines, and I found it soothing. Others might consider it a kind of slavery, but I really did feel that I was my own boss, and when I was finished the work at the end of the day, and looked at the sparkling office, I felt a kind of satisfaction that my customers would start the new day in a fresh environment. I also saw a unique opportunity for creating an independent business. I took a week's holiday, which I used to look for contracts. I was successful. I found contracts that brought me in $1,500 a month, which was pretty decent money at the time. I handed in my resignation as a lathe operator, and from that moment on, I devoted myself to cleaning full time.

The claim that he really enjoyed cleaning is interesting for a surprising reason. Milan came from what, under normal circumstances, would have been a fairly successful European middle-class family, who would have considered certain kinds of work beneath them, though it was not unusual in a Communist state to see a former factory owner cleaning toilets, just as in Canada no one is surprised to find a university professor from Afghanistan driving a taxi. The fact that Milan found satisfaction in cleaning buildings shows he was not trapped by his background and was able to recognize that Canada was a new world, and that how you make your living is far less important there than in the "old world."

Milan had just grasped the biggest star in his life so far. His father would have been delighted.

M & L OFFICE MAINTENANCE
CO.

Bus: 536-4884
Res: 532-8992

77 Spencer Ave.
Toronto 150, Ont.

MILAN KROUPA

The Apprenticeship of a Canadian Entrepreneur

MILAN DID NOT ENTER the Canadian entrepreneurial arena completely unprepared.

Though he may not have realized it, his father's advice was quietly fermenting within him. The metaphor of the stars, and his father's own ventures into entrepreneurship — making paintbrush handles from scrap wood, raising livestock, manufacturing cinder blocks, cutting the community grass for hay, repairing old machinery, some of which, under the Communist regime, had cost him another prison term — as well as Milan's own struggle with the authorities over the kind of work he was willing to do: all of this shaped his outlook. He had also kept alive the inspiration he had gained from the novel he'd been so reluctant to read, *In the Glow of Millions*.

FACING

Milan's first business card.

About three months after the invasion of Czechoslovakia, however, his first entrepreneurial act in Canada was unexpectedly complicated by the arrival of his brother, Lad'a, and Lad'a's wife, Miluška. When they arrived in Toronto, Milan wanted to impress them by taking them, in his rusty Volkswagen, straight from the airport to a doughnut shop. Milan himself had never eaten a Canadian doughnut before, so he ordered the most impressive-looking doughnuts and found, from the very first bite, that he disliked them intensely! At the doughnut shop, Lad'a informed Milan his mistress would soon be coming to join them as well. When she arrived, Miluška refused to live in a ménage à trois, so Milan found her a flat of her own.

That was not the end of Milan's family complications. Milan felt responsible for helping his brother, so he brought him into his cleaning company, even though he knew Lad'a had bought into the slack Communist work ethic and was not that keen on making much of an effort. He registered the firm under the name M & L Office Maintenance and drew up an agreement with Lad'a, according to which each of them would look after half of the cleaning contracts, and Milan (who cleaned at night) would also spend the days looking for new customers.

Every morning, when he came into their modest office, at the corner of Davenport and Bay, Milan would open Scott's Directory, which listed addresses and telephone numbers of companies in Toronto, looking for small and midsized firms he would have the capacity to service. One by one, he contacted the most likely prospects and offered them his services. Every day, he called on the manager or owner of at least five companies — twenty-five a week. He got roughly one new client for every one hundred attempts.

It was an activity he loved: "Rejection never discouraged me. I saw each encounter with a prospective client as a learning experience and a chance to polish my presentation. The more refusals I had, the more it pushed me to improve myself, and I was spurred on by the feeling that I was never doing enough. Part of the problem was that I didn't yet know how to estimate the value of my work properly, and I set my prices very low. In this way, my company grew slowly, but surely."

About a year later, Lad'a asked Milan to pay Lad'a's mistress, Mimina, who was also working for the firm, a higher salary. Milan refused: they had divided the work into two equal halves; Lad'a and Mimina looked after one half, and Milan did the rest and spent his days acquiring new contracts for the firm. Lad'a didn't want to see it that way and became very upset. It was not a good tactic. Milan told Lad'a he would think it over, but he already knew what his answer would be. That afternoon, he registered a second company also called M and L Office Maintenance, with this difference: he made himself the sole owner. (Nowadays, it would be impossible to register a second firm under the same name, but back then he got away with it.) The following day, he told Lad'a he'd turn his half of the business over to him, but that would be the end of their partnership. "You see, Lad'a, we're very different," Milan told him. "I haven't the strength any more to argue with you over every new idea. You're holding me back, and I think that I'll get ahead faster without you." And, in fact, he did.

One reason for this was the fact that Milan had managed to get a look inside the Toronto cleaning business. Initially, he had to buy contracts from the bosses of the main cleaning firm for $12,000. He paid half up front and the remaining $6,000 over the duration of the contract. When he had paid everything off, the bosses went to the owner of the building Milan had been cleaning and offered to clean the building for a lower rate. When the owner agreed, the bosses told Milan his contract was terminated because — so they claimed — the customer was dissatisfied with his work. Then they sold the contract to another "Milan."

How had he figured this out? Suspecting something wasn't right, he waited one evening in front of an ex-customer's building. In a while, a familiar truck approached the building and one of the bosses got out, accompanied by the new "Milan" to whom he'd re-sold the contract. Milan tried to confront the boss, but before he had a chance to say anything, the boss lit into him: "Milan, I don't want any trouble. Come into the office tomorrow and we'll sort it out."

Milan was surprised by the boss's reaction, but he kept his temper and left without a word. On the way home, he said to himself: "So that's how they help new entrepreneurs be their own boss!" The next morning, he went to their office. They kept him waiting for a long time, clearly trying to discourage him from confronting them. Their tactics reminded Milan of how Communist prison guards and the secret police treated people. One of the bosses finally summoned him into his office and very curtly told him he'd done the work badly and had no right to any compensation. Milan turned around without a word and left the office. But that wasn't the end of it: "On the way out, I hatched a plan," Milan says.

I pulled out copies of about a dozen contracts I had fulfilled but which were invoiced to the firm I'd bought the contracts from — my old "bosses." I discovered that there was no exclusivity clause in the contracts to prevent me from taking on the customers for myself. So I rewrote all the contracts, making the fees directly payable to my own firm. It was a lot of work because each contract was several pages long and I had to type each one myself on a borrowed typewriter. But that was how I managed to save the remaining contracts.

The next day, I dressed smartly and asked for meetings with the presidents of the firms whose contracts I had rewritten. I explained how the fraud that the "bosses" had perpetrated worked and offered to work directly for them. With one exception, all of them agreed to sign with me. At first my original "bosses" wanted to take me to court, but they backed off when they discovered that, without an exclusivity clause, they had no chance of winning.

It was a brilliant coup for a new Canadian who had been in the country for only a couple of years, who didn't yet know English very well, and who had spent his youth chasing either a soccer ball or girls, that is when the girls weren't chasing him.

After two years, Milan was able to move his family into an attractive modern flat in Mississauga and replace the rusty old Volkswagen with something better — a Renault. But even though Milan had drummed up more work than he could handle himself and had to hire a couple of cleaners, he was still not satisfied. He had come to realize he simply did not have enough experience to deal effectively with his customers or train his employees. He didn't even know how to pay them properly. And although his most important entrepreneurial skill was his ability to get new customers, he correctly concluded:

As long as that skill isn't supported by the quality of the work and the reliability of well-trained employees, everything could ultimately fall apart. I also realized that I was in over my head, since I really had no idea what it took to build a successful company. So I left the back door open and instead of devoting myself 100 percent to improving myself within my own company, I remained open to other opportunities. One of them proved to be so attractive that I forgot my father's advice. I let go of the star I already held in my hand and went chasing off after another.

Pumping Gas and Slinging Burgers

ONE OF MILAN'S IMMIGRANT FRIENDS was an excellent mechanic by the name of Emil. He owned an auto repair shop and kept Milan's car in good running condition. During one of his visits, the two of them started talking and Emil told Milan he had found a gold mine. It was about 240 kilometres north of Toronto, close to the town of Port Severn in Muskoka, a recreational area where wealthy and successful people from all over the world go for weekends, often spending the whole summer there.

"There's a gas station for sale there that has a garage, a little restaurant, and a souvenir shop attached to it," Emil said. "It's an unbelievable opportunity. Let's go into business together."

Still somewhat unsure of his readiness to run a larger company, Milan ignored his father's advice, let go of the cleaning company, sold his contracts for $15,000, and used the money as a down payment on the restaurant and the souvenir shop.

Emil took over the gas station and the garage; Milan looked after the restaurant and the gift shop. Both of them saw a great future ahead. The businesses were strategically located in a spot where the Ontario government was constructing a new multi-lane highway that would greatly increase the tourist traffic. They imagined crowds of tourists who, after buying T-shirts and baseball caps, would enjoy chowing down on Milan's hamburgers while waiting for Emil to repair their cars.

The two men divided up the work, but they also helped each other out. Both businesses were open twenty-four hours a day. Milan found himself flipping hamburgers on the grill one moment and pumping gas outside the next. He was inordinately proud of his hamburgers: "Our burgers were outstanding because they had a particular smell of gasoline about them, which most of our customers could not appreciate, but which I considered 'romantic.'"

When Milan and his family moved to Port Severn, they had been in Canada for five years. By now, he and Milena had two children. Robert was five and his younger brother was three.

At the time of the new baby's conception, the family lived on Spencer Avenue in the Toronto neighbourhood of Parkdale, just around the corner from Cowan Avenue, where the Czechoslovak social centre, Masaryk Hall, used to be. Today, the building is still a social centre and still carries Masaryk's name, as does an adjacent parkette. Since then, however, the Czech and Slovak community centre has moved to Scarborough.

In June 1969, the married couple had a conversation that is worth recording (at least as Milan remembers it):

It was one early morning in 1969, Milena and I were lying in bed, the picture of marital bliss, when Milena casually remarked: "If I were to get pregnant today, what month would the child be born in? My goodness, it would be February, the same month as you were born in!" My vanity couldn't resist. "All right," I said. "Let's go for it."

Nine months later, Milena had a very round belly. One February day, she was standing in the kitchen getting little Robert something to eat when her waters broke. I drove her straight to the maternity ward at St. Joseph's Hospital in the west end of Toronto, and then went back to look after Robert. Robert had a cot in one bedroom, which the new mother was meant to occupy. Before the baby was born, Milena and I slept on a folding couch in the living room. About five in the morning, on the day that Milena was going to bring the baby home, I was asleep on the folding couch. I heard Robert climbing out of his cot and beginning his daily assaults on our flat. Since I knew that this was my last chance to sleep in peace before Milena and the baby arrived, I left Robert to his own devices and went back to sleep. It was a big mistake. Having often observed his mother cracking eggs for breakfast, Robert had managed to turn on the gas, find some eggs in the fridge, pull up a chair, and crack open the eggs over a burning element. But he forgot one detail — the frying pan. When the eggs hit the stove, my sweet dreams were suddenly interrupted by a terrible smell. I flew off the couch, put the fire out, ventilated the kitchen, and when things were more or less under control, I set off with a smile on my face to the hospital to pick up Milena and the baby.

They called the latest family member Michael.

The gas bar in Port Severn was not one of Milan's most successful business ventures. Besides working in the restaurant and the souvenir shop, and tending the pumps, he also kept the books. He put money in the bank, and every month he paid the bills. He had a good overview of the returns from the shop, the restaurant, and the gas pumps, but he had no insight into the finances of the garage, which was Emil's exclusive domain. One night, when Milan was working the pumps and tending to the restaurant, several policemen showed up and asked Milan to help tow a car that had rolled over a short distance from the garage. Milan didn't want to wake up Emil, so he got Milena out of bed to look after the pumps and the restaurant, and he climbed into Emil's tow truck. While reaching under the seat to adjust it, he found several twenty-dollar bills. He also found a bottle of liquor in the side pocket. He drove to the site of the accident and managed to right the car, but the tow truck stalled and could not be restarted, so he was unable to remove the car from the scene. It reminded him of the old adage about the blacksmith's horse going unshod: Emil serviced cars for people in the area, but he didn't take proper care of his own. Clearly, he also had a drinking problem. The police didn't say anything, but they never again turned to Milan and Emil for help. The two entrepreneurs lost a good customer.

Milan knew that Emil drank. He also knew he had some pretty violent quarrels with his wife, a woman who could make eloquent use of street Czech. Her unstoppable flow once reached such a pitch of intensity Emil threw a large kitchen knife at her. She ducked with surprising agility, and the knife stuck in the wall behind her. In the interest of truth, it must be said that Emil's wife did not eschew physical force either: once, when Emil was roaring drunk, she beat him so badly his face was covered in bruises. Neither of them really cared much who saw or heard their battles.

Among those who did see and hear them was Milena. She didn't think the couple's behaviour would have a positive influence on her marriage and was worried about how it might affect the children. When Milena was unhappy about something, Milan soon heard about it.

After eight months, she came to me and said, quite calmly, "I know you like it here, but it's not a healthy place for me and the boys. You can stay if you like, but I'm packing my bags and taking the children back to Toronto."

"No," I replied. "We came here as a family and that's how we're going to leave." I packed as much as I could into a small truck and then went to settle up with Emil. I knew he was a crude man, and that he would be incapable of coming up with a fair settlement, so I was frank with him: "I'm leaving now with my family. You owe me $6,000. I know that you can't pay me right now, but I know that you eventually will." Emil got mad, but eventually we settled on the terms of separation. Fortunately, I'd been making fairly decent money, enough to provide for my family for a short time at least.

Another incident with Milan's brother, Laďa, happened about this time: "During our stay in Port Severn," Milan recalls, "Laďa and Mimina would occasionally come to visit. Once, Laďa took me aside and said: 'Mimina's really getting on my nerves. Couldn't you help me dump her? I've got myself a new girl.' I sorted the situation out by giving Mimina a job as a waitress in the restaurant. Laďa left without her and went back to Toronto alone, where he began working as an electrician. The abandoned Mimina cried her eyes out on the shoulders of a muscular young man, Pepíček, who was also working for us in the restaurant. The next morning, they woke up in bed together, and some time later, Pepíček married Mimina. Today, they have a son who is a lawyer."

Tryouts

EVEN THOUGH MILAN'S FAMILY didn't return to Toronto empty-handed, both he and Milena knew that in Toronto they would have to do better than before, when Milan occasionally made $1,000 a week, though most of the time it was less. "Today, people only see Milan's success," Milena says, "but very few know that there were many sleepless nights and a lot of stress and uncertainty about whether we could afford milk for the children the next day. And even though Milan knew that when the government support ended we could ask for social assistance, he was too proud to do that. He would rather have cleaned day and night."

Milena started working as a waitress, and in the evenings, Milan scanned the want ads for employment. One evening, he saw a company called Albert White, Office Furniture and Stationery Limited was looking for someone to manage several commercial buildings in the trendy Toronto neighbourhood around Queen and Spadina. The next day, he telephoned Mr. White and gave an upbeat account of his experience as the owner of a restaurant in Port Severn and in cleaning commercial buildings. He thought there couldn't be that much difference between a cleaner, a manager, and a janitor, and he also thought Mr. White couldn't help but be impressed by the passion with which Milan talked about his experience. But after hearing him out, Mr. White concluded Milan was not right for the job and told him so. Milan responded with characteristic persuasiveness and passion: "Mr. White, how can you turn me down when you haven't even seen me? Give me a chance to talk to you personally. I'm telling you, I can do this job."

Mr. White invited Milan for a fifteen-minute meeting in his office at 67 Spadina Avenue. The meeting lasted an hour. Milan presented himself as an adaptable and ambitious man and eventually convinced Mr. White to give him a chance. "I can't pay you much," he said. "You're inexperienced and uneducated, and you don't have the qualifications for the job." He offered Milan a salary that was pretty meagre at the time — one hundred dollars a week. Milan accepted. He saw it as an opportunity to get the organizational experience he lacked. It would be like going to school for free.

For the first couple of weeks, the previous manager, a Mr. Deutsch, instructed him. However, Deutsch left soon after that, and Milan now had the opportunity to show what he could do on his own. One of his first and most important jobs was to transform a warehouse into a showroom where clothing merchants could bring their customers — shop owners or buyers for boutiques and department stores — and show them selections for the new season. The business set the fashion trends in Toronto. For Milan, it was a fascinating new environment:

I was no longer spending my time alone at night in empty offices, and I learned a lot from the diversity of the customers, their requirements, and their approach to business. In this way I gained valuable knowledge I would need for my future enterprises. In the meantime, I also had to collect the rents, and in the process, I learned how to deal with people in a variety of circumstances. In one of the offices we had a tenant who owed three months' back rent. At the beginning of the fourth month, when I knocked on his door and asked for the rent, he almost burst into tears: "I don't have the money; I didn't sell anything last month. But I'm convinced my luck will change, and I'll be able to pay next month."

He ended with an appeal to Milan's fatherly instincts: "I've got two children to look after." He used the right tactic. Milan promised to wait until the next month.

When he walked past the glass-walled office of Mr. White, the boss called him in: "So, how's it going with the rents?" Milan was so carried away by his own generosity, he gave his boss an emotional account of how nobly he had behaved towards the indebted tenant. Mr. White was not impressed. He leapt out of his chair and shouted: "That's my money you're talking about! How can you possibly handle my money that way?"

Milan could see his boss's point. When Mr. White stopped shouting, Milan left his office and sat on the staircase, thinking he'd probably be fired, particularly when he saw Mr. White approaching him. But by this time, Mr. White had calmed down. Instead of firing Milan, he invited him back into his office, looked at him for a long time, and then in a friendly manner said: "Milan, you're a very good lad, but I don't know what to do with you." Milan remembered a tactic he had learned in the refugee camp: admit your error and move on. "Mr. White," he said, "I realize I made a mistake. Give me two weeks and I'll improve."

The boss tacitly accepted my offer, and as he was walking away, I called after him: "Mr. White, could you tell me what you'd have done in my place?" He stopped, thought for a while, and then replied: "Meet me here tomorrow morning, at eight o'clock."

The next morning at eight o'clock Mr. White was standing with a janitor outside the door of the tenant who owed him money. The janitor was fitting a new padlock on the door. Mr. White told Milan to go into his own office and wait.

So I was sitting there, thinking things over, when all of a sudden, around eleven o'clock, someone knocked on my door. At my invitation the tenant walked in with a cheque in his hand, looking sheepish. He threw it on the table in front of me. It was a certified cheque covering the rent for the previous three months and the rent for the coming month. "You lied to me!" I said. "You had the money all along! How could you lie to me?"

The tenant looked at me and replied with icy calm, "It's business," and walked out.

"You idiot!" I said to myself. It was all a game for him. It taught me you can't take things personally and bleed for every cause. The rules of business are like the rules of soccer. You've got to obey them and uncompromisingly play your position so your team can depend on you. Even though you may feel sorry for your opponent, it's your responsibility to stop him from scoring a goal.

In the next two weeks, Milan was able to show Mr. White he could be a valuable team player. One of Milan's responsibilities was to make drawings of all the proposed changes to the interior spaces of the buildings and then take the finished plans to city hall for approval. Coincidentally, he had met a young woman who was skilled at drawing up blueprints. As a result, he had found himself in another argument with Mr. White, because he had promised her remuneration Mr. White thought was too generous. Milan's solution was to learn from her how to make the appropriate drawings himself, thus saving Mr. White a lot of money. He never asked Mr. White for a raise in his own meagre pay, and Mr. White never offered.

Three months later, Mr. White came to Milan with an interesting offer: "Milan, I think you've got a bright future ahead of you. Whenever I have a meeting with new prospects, or with my current tenants regarding their contracts, I'd like you to sit in. I don't want you to take part, just sit in the corner, keep your mouth shut, and watch what I do."

"It was more valuable than a university education," Milan says. "Albert White was a master in dealing with people. He knew exactly what to offer the person in question, when to back down, and when he could ask for more. It was a combination of natural talent and long experience, and watching him was like watching a star soccer or hockey player. Several weeks later, he invited me to take part in the negotiations. Afterwards, he would go over it with me a couple of times, suggest improvements, and finally, he let me do the negotiating myself. I felt as though I were passing my university entrance exam. At the same time, though, I became more and more certain that my future did not lie with Albert White."

During his time with Albert White, Milan cultivated relationships with various tradesmen who did repair jobs for the company. He ended up signing a contract to work for Garney and Company Limited, a firm that installed heating and air conditioning. Milan didn't have the courage to tell Mr. White to his face that he was leaving. He wrote a letter of resignation, thanking him for everything he had done for him and giving two weeks' notice. He put the letter on Mr. White's desk and went to oversee tradesmen on another floor. A little while later, Mr. White came for him, spoke very flatteringly of him, then offered him a raise.

But Milan had already made up his mind. After the two-week period was up, he started working for Garney and Company.

He enjoyed his new job. He had always liked working with his hands, and he made enough money that Milena didn't have to go out to work. Life unfolded peacefully, perhaps a little too peacefully. Then Milan decided to help out his brother, who was once again having problems. They had not spoken to each other for several years, but Milan thought if he could change, there was no reason why Lad'a couldn't change as well, particularly because his new love interest was a very capable and sympathetic German woman. Milan got his employers to agree to hire Lad'a as a member of his installation team.

The first project they worked on together, however, did not turn out well: "I showed Lad'a how to measure the system for new pipes, drawing everything in chalk. Lad'a stood leaning against the wall, smoking a cigarette — back then you could smoke anywhere — and finally he looked at me and said, 'The way you're going about it is stupid! We won't do it that way.'"

That was the beginning of the end for Lad'a's time with Garney and Company Limited, and ultimately it was Milan's end as well. Even though he enjoyed the work and made good money, he wasn't entirely satisfied. The business of installing heating and cooling systems seemed complicated, from both a technical and organizational point of view. The work demanded continual innovation, yet the quality of the results depended on the skill and experience of the installers, the reliability of the suppliers, and the eccentric demands of the customers. Too many things could go wrong.

Something was pulling him back towards cleaning. Technically and organizationally, cleaning seemed to Milan far simpler; it offered an independence he didn't see in other fields, and if he owned his own firm, in a pinch, he could always do the work himself. Yet he didn't feel quite ready to start his own firm: the gaps in his experience were still too large, and there was still too much he didn't know about running a firm, negotiating contracts, and organizing and motivating the employees. But he had to start somewhere.

"One day, I sat down and patched together a resumé that I sent to about twenty large cleaning firms. The only one that replied was Gordon A. McEachern, a highly reputable company that had contracts to clean offices and stores all across Canada. The grocery giant Loblaws was one of its biggest customers. Gordon A. McEachern Limited was looking for the right person to fill the position of operations manager, a job that involved coordinating their expansive network. I still have a copy of my resumé, and it's both funny and embarrassing to see how lousy it was. At the time, I saw nothing to worry about. My only interest was in an opportunity to learn more."

Milan's interview with a spokesman for McEachern Limited took place in the firm's glass-walled offices on the second floor of a building on McCaul Street not far from Albert White's building.

"I will never forget that conversation," Milan says.

The company's spokesman was an imposing man with a pronounced English accent, who took a keen interest in my experience. I felt that the conversation was going well, so I relaxed and talked freely. My impression was not wrong. At the end of the conversation the man immediately offered me a job and introduced me to my future colleagues, including my immediate superior, a Yugoslav of Croatian origin by the name of Joe Grguric, who was about to be promoted from the position for which I was now being hired. I liked that. Not only because they were hiring immigrants, but they were also giving them the opportunity to move up the ladder. At first, Joe regarded me with a certain wariness, but I knew it wouldn't be long before I would show him what I could do.

Milan started work two weeks later. It was a new chapter in his life. He was given a company car and paid well, and also gained a certain prestige. Joe Grguric showed him the ropes, but Milan quickly discovered they had very different opinions on how to run the department. Joe tried to get Milan to do everything the same way as he had done it; Milan wanted to implement his own ideas as soon as he could. One day, he turned to Joe and said (their desks were in the same office): "'Could you do me a great favour? Throw me into the water and let me swim. I need you to give me more room to do things my own way.' Joe looked at me in surprise. 'Are you sure?' he said. He couldn't believe that after only two weeks on the job anyone would have the confidence and the nerve to ask for the freedom to manage an important department without supervision. Perhaps because it only involved Toronto, he granted my request. From then on, he never had to worry about my work. I dealt with all the problems that came up myself."

Shortly after that, Joe gave Milan the opportunity to really show what he could do by assigning him to look after a large building in North York. It was a new contract, and the top managers estimated they would need about thirty cleaners to cover it. Naturally, Joe was curious about how Milan would handle this contract.

"One day, he sent me on a tour of the building so that I could put together a proposal for a cleaning system. The next day, he came to see how I'd done. When I took him through the building and explained my strategic plan, he looked at me for the first time with respect: 'You're good! You're going to work out.'"

Learning Curve

MILAN LEARNED A LOT during his employment with McEachern. He learned, for example, how enterprises made money. McEachern's earning capacity was based on two revenue streams. The first came from providing cleaning services to commercial buildings and chain stores with branches across the country; the second came from manufacturing cleaning products. As a manager, Milan had the opportunity to study the financial structure of both branches of the firm. What he saw did not inspire confidence.

"The cleaning products division was much neglected," Milan says. "McEachern had set up a chemical factory to make these products, but because he was focussed on his cleaning services, he under-invested in the factory and, over time, lost his competitive edge. When I looked at the books, I found that we were losing $50,000 a month on the production side. The cleaning services were clearing approximately $27,000 a month so, although my department was doing well, it was pretty easy to see that I had found myself on a sinking ship."

As Milan saw it, the earnings of the cleaning department were nothing to write home about either. There were several reasons for this: no one had ever properly analyzed the contracts to see why some were earning money and others were not; no one had worked out a system to maximize profits. Furthermore, clients were scattered all across Canada but never in such concentrations that would enable the firm to make the best use of its resources. On top of that, the firm lacked aggressive leadership: old Mr. McEachern no longer had the necessary interest or energy. McEachern's successor, his son Alex, had, according to Milan, "studied psychology and had a basic intelligence and a feeling for people. He was a good person to talk to — but he was lacking in good business instincts. He hired consultants to advise him on the best way out of the situation, and I also tried to advise him, but he had serious blind spots."

During one conversation with Alex, Milan suggested one way to improve the profitability would be to shut down the cleaning product factories. Milan remembers Alex's response very well: "'Milan, I won't even consider that. Every time I go into a Dominion store, it warms my heart to see bottles with the McEachern name on the labels.' That was when I understood that Alex's ego had trumped his business acumen."

The two men had a confidential meeting again after the death of old Mr. McEachern. Alex wanted to know what Milan was doing to make his department so productive. Milan mentioned several factors, but shortly after that he had the opportunity to demonstrate his know-how. The firm had a contract with Inco Limited in Manitoba that brought in $50,000 a month before expenses. But the client was not satisfied with the quality of the work and was threatening to cancel the contract. Alex's advisors said: "Send in Kroupa."

When Milan arrived in Manitoba, a consultant was waiting for him and introduced him to a representative of Inco. They gave Milan two weeks to analyze the problem and work out a way to solve it. Two weeks later, Milan handed in the analysis and his plan for improvement, and according to Milan, a sympathetic middle-aged gentleman, who turned out to be the CEO, spoke out. This would be one of the high points in Milan's professional life. "He pointed at me and said, 'If this fellow is going to be supervising the contract, then we'll keep McEachern on as our cleaning service.'"

That, too, was an answer to Alex's question about why Milan's department was doing so well: the main reason was Milan.

Milan remembers another episode that happened shortly after his Manitoba triumph. Alex invited all the managers into his office, including the chief operations manager, Jack. As Milan remembers it:

Alex announced that he was terminating Jack and I would be taking his place, effective immediately. So I became McEachern's chief manager of operating systems for the whole of Canada, but the promotion also gave me pause. Jack was a very knowledgeable fellow with a great deal of experience and had done a lot for the firm. At that moment, I realized the same thing could happen to me. That strengthened my resolve to establish my own firm. Even though I had no immediate plans to leave the McEacherns — after all, it was old Mr. McEachern who had given me the chance to work in such a prestigious company in the first place — I wanted to be prepared for every eventuality. I now felt that I was holding in my hands most of the pieces I needed to put together my future enterprises.

I found one of the final pieces at Humber College when I signed up for a three-year evening course in the psychology of management. I was surprised to discover that I had already been making instinctive use of many of the strategies they were teaching. The course allowed me to become fully conscious of my methods, to polish them, and to file them away in my brain. Naturally, I learned new things as well. Compared to the other students, however, I had the advantage of practical experience, and thanks to my high position in the firm, I was able to try out the theories I learned at school in real situations. I no longer had to ask anyone for the chance to prove myself, and my self-confidence rapidly increased.

It was time for Milan to make his big move.

I called it United Cleaning Services Limited. It had three shareholders, who were also board members: myself, Ron Macari, a man of Uruguayan origin who was a close colleague of mine and a co-worker, and a Canadian army retiree from London, Ontario, who later changed his mind and decided to stay with McEachern, although his name remained on the registration form. I told no one about registering the new firm, but employees of the cleaning products factory, who regularly visited the registration office to get names of cleaning companies to offer their products to, noticed the registration of my firm.

One day, I returned from a business trip to Thunder Bay, and on the way to my office, I met Alex McEachern. He pretended not to see me, although up till then we'd had a very warm relationship. But as soon as I entered my office, Alex literally flew into the room and started right in: "What in the world are you thinking? Do you have any idea what you're doing? You simply can't do that to us! Cancel the registration of your firm at once and we'll just say it never happened."

Instead, I gave him my two weeks' notice. In the next two weeks, the pressure mounted, not just on me but on my partner Ron Macari as well. In the end, Ron capitulated and stayed with McEachern. But I would not be moved. I had grasped a new star, and I knew that I mustn't let go of it at any price. Ron Macari took my place at McEachern. First, however, he had to sign a document saying he was no longer a partner in my firm. I remember how he sat in my car with a pen in his hand, and he looked me in the eye and said, "I know I'm going to regret this for the rest of my life."

The contacts Milan had made with the firm's clients turned out to be more important than the experience he had gained. His most important contact for the future of his new company was a national grocery chain. At McEachern, they had a system for cleaning their stores that they called "Truck Run."

It was a mobile service consisting of six guys with cleaning machines in a van that went out at night to clean the stores. Each mobile group cleaned four stores a night, three times a week. I managed these groups. One day, in 1974, Joe sent me to meet a company manager to end the contract. He said it wasn't earning enough money for us. I immediately saw an opportunity to shine. I proposed that instead of cancelling the contract, they give me the chance to find a way to make money with the client. By this time, Joe trusted me. "Give it a try," Joe said.

"How long are you going to give me to do this?"

"Take a year!"

So, I drew up a working schedule in which every cleaner had a very specific role, like soccer players on a team. My role was coach. Every evening at eleven o'clock, I met with the cleaners and gave them my schedule and, with the leader of each group, went over their responsibilities, so it would be clear to everyone. At eleven o'clock in the evening, I would meet with them before they left for work, and I would be waiting for them when they came back at seven in the morning, when I held a debriefing session to go over any problems or suggestions for improvement.

I don't think anyone had ever shown that level of commitment before. But it fascinated me for strategic reasons. When I really got into the nitty-gritty of how these mobile groups worked, it wasn't long before I found several ways to improve their efficiency. For example, the main reason why every team had six cleaners was because, on average, only three of them would show up for work. The other three would often just stay at home without giving any prior warning. Also, they weren't very productive. No one checked up on them. They made an average of $1.40 an hour, and they could easily make that elsewhere, so they had no reason to work hard. I decided to introduce discipline and responsibility into the work.

150

The mathematics of Milan's new budget were simple. Having determined that three men per team were enough to get the job done, he chose the three best workers from each group and let the others go. He divided the pay of two of the men he'd fired among the remaining three and gave the remaining third back to the firm. In this way, he killed two birds with one stone. The better-paid employees did better work, not only because they were making more money, but also because they felt Milan valued them, and they began to take pride in work that was well done and fairly paid.

Milan's brilliant solution was a hit with his boss, and if he had a problem with letting the superfluous workers go, his conscience was eased by the knowledge they would easily find other work. It was like a soccer team — there was no longer a position on the team for them — and perhaps most persuasively, he remembered what he'd learned from Mr. White's tenant: "It's business." So when the time came, he summoned all six mobile groups on the carpet, stood them on a platform where they stored the cleaning machines, pulled out a piece of paper with a list of names, and said: "Anyone whose name I read out, please go to the other side of the room and wait. If you don't hear your name, you can go home."

> *And so I fired half my employees, eighteen in all. Only one of them objected and started threatening me. "If you don't leave, I'm going to call the police," I said, as calmly as I could. When he saw that there was nothing he could do, he finally left. From that moment on, our productivity greatly increased. My team made the most money for the firm, and Loblaws offered us contracts to clean several more stores.*

Thus began the cooperation between Loblaws and Milan. It would come to play an important role in his own firm's future.

The Uncertain Debut of United Cleaning Services Limited

IT BEGAN IN EUPHORIA. After leaving McEachern, Milan felt as light as a bird as he drove home, dreaming about his future as an independent entrepreneur. But the sight of the envelope on the seat beside him with his final paycheque in it quickly brought him back down to earth. He was on his own now, though of course he had Milena's full support. But in the meantime, they had bought a house and had mortgage payments to keep up. There was a lot at stake.

The beginnings of United Cleaning Services were very modest. I rented my first "office" from my former employer, the one for whom I had once installed heating and air-conditioning systems. It was a modest place in a basement, more like an underground lair. I discovered just how damp and unhealthy the conditions were when the paper clips I used to organize my documents would

A United Cleaning Services employee at work.

rust overnight. Clearly, the ventilation system wasn't working. My desk was the height of luxury: a slab of plywood spanning two crates that were miraculously the same height. When I needed an inclined surface to draw up plans, I used three containers of floor wax on each side at the rear and two on each side at the front.

On my second day in the office I saw the world in a somewhat more sober light: "You idiot!" I said to myself. "Yesterday, you had a secretary, a beautiful car, and the respect of the bosses of one of the most successful cleaning companies in Canada. Yesterday, you were a star, and today you are a zero." But at the same time, I also realized that I was my own *zero, and it was up to me to make something of myself. I had to establish myself at any cost, and if it didn't work out, no one could fire me.*

At that time, two powerful emotional forces were battling it out within Milan. On the one hand, he knew he had bitten off a very big mouthful: he had thrown down the gauntlet before a large well-known company without having a single customer or the backing of a single investor. On the other hand, he was aware if he approached some of his former clients, they would probably come over to him, but it didn't seem right — even though, if his back were to the wall, he would probably have managed to surmount that barrier. At the same time, he had to deal with the problem of the non-compete clause he had signed as part of his severance agreement with McEachern.

The validity of that clause was soon put to the test when some of his former customers approached him and offered him contracts. Milan won the resulting lawsuit with a very short and unconventional argument that had nothing to do with the legal issues involved: "I didn't have much choice," he told the judge. "I'm an immigrant,

I wasn't educated here, and this is the only way I know to support my family."

Since then, Milan has viewed non-compete clauses as an ethical issue in conflict with the basic principles of capitalism. Competition was something that inspired him. It impelled his boundless faith in himself, a faith driven by qualities such as pride, vanity, and stubbornness, but also exceptional talent, vision, and a sportsmanlike compulsion to win. Milan knew he could win. Yet what if he didn't? Who would look after his family?

When he was at his lowest ebb, he ran into his old buddy Joe Grguric. Milan confessed he was losing his appetite for business. He was having trouble financing the company and was afraid his family would suffer as a result. Joe advised him not to give up, but if he didn't feel up to running a company on his own, perhaps he should try to find a job. Milan looked for other work. He was offered a position at $15,000 a year, but since he had been making $27,000 a year with McEachern, plus a car and perks, he turned it down. That was the end of his search for other employment.

As often happens to Milan when he doesn't know which way to turn, help arrived out of the blue. He met a young man who had recently been let go from McEachern and was now working with two colleagues who were acting as business consultants. Milan told him about his financial problems. The young man advised him to draw up a business plan for his new company and offered to show it to his colleagues.

The budget Milan prepared showed no profit for the first three months, and factored in a salary for Milan of $2,700 a month in his first year, which was the minimum he needed to support his family and pay the mortgage on the house. The mortgage was a key item because a week after his departure from McEachern, the bank notified him they

Some of the United Cleaning Services fleet in front of the offices on Norseman Street, Toronto.

Milan and his father in the Norseman Street office, 1979.

wouldn't renew it because he'd lost his job, which could lead to the loss of his house. He also projected a profit for his company of $25,000 in the second year. The financial planners were impressed and decided to invest in the company. In addition to lending him $15,000 at prime and acting as his guarantors, when he told them the bank was refusing to renew his mortgage, they sent the bank a letter saying that Milan was employed by them, thus in effect underwriting his mortgage.

Having arranged for proper financing, Milan rented a better office on Norseman Street in the west end of Toronto, near the intersection of Kipling and Bloor. The location provided convenient access to many commercial buildings that might become potential clients, and he approached several companies a day, but his success rate, as before, was only one in a hundred. His biggest problem was getting past the receptionists to see their bosses. Once again, fate came to the rescue.

At that time, he would occasionally stop in for a beer at the Mountain Hut on the corner of Church and Dundas, a pub run by a Czech called Mr. Puhlovský. On one occasion, he struck up a conversation with Pavel Kantorek, a Czech who had made a name for himself in Communist Czechoslovakia as a cartoonist for the popular humour magazine *Dikobraz*.

> *After a short conversation, I made a suggestion. I told Pavel I needed a funny brochure that would help me get past the wall of secretaries. The brochure, as I described it to him, would be on standard letter-sized paper folded in three. On the first panel, you see dirty footprints on a floor; on the second panel, you see a little man operating a cleaning machine and the footprints on the floor are half-gone; on the third panel, the floor behind the little man is sparkling clean. Pavel made the cartoon for me in his own inimitable style.*

Dear Customer;

We are a company realizing that only sincerity with our customers and quality service will lead us to success.

Give us the opportunity to prove ourselves, we will appreciate your business.

United Cleaning Services Limited

Armed with this drawing, I no longer needed to beg for a hearing but would enter the reception area and announce, authoritatively, "Miss, I represent the new cleaning service, and I urgently need to talk to your boss. I have important information for him. Here's our brochure."

I would hand her Kantorek's cartoon. The receptionist wouldn't want to be responsible for her boss missing a potentially important meeting, and in most cases, the brochure made her laugh, and before she realized what she was doing, she'd tell me her boss's name. After that, everything went smoothly, and I began to get new contracts. If they already had a cleaning service, naturally it didn't work out, but there was no ill will. That simple device gave me the advantage of surprise and humour, and humour raised the level of the game. As soon as people laugh, you've got their attention and it's far harder for them to slam the door in your face.

JANITORIAL SERVICES
WINDOW CLEANING
CARPET CLEANING
WALL WASHING
SECURITY SERVICE

When we say clean,

that's what we mean!

ABOVE

*The UCS
brochure
illustrated
by Pavel
Kantorek.*

LEFT

*When they
say clean,
that's what
they mean.*

159

Six or seven months after Milan's departure from McEachern, Ron Macari showed up in his office. He complained that the McEacherns weren't treating him very well and that he wanted to work for Milan instead. Milan was wary, but in the end he decided to give Ron a second chance, not as a partner (he'd had to withdraw as a partner in Milan's firm to stay with McEachern), but as an employee. About a month later, this move seemed almost like foresight. One day, while playing soccer in the back garden with his sons, Milan broke his ankle.

"It was a bad break," Milan remembers. "It was Easter, and I was lying in the emergency ward for a long time, waiting for surgery. I was desperate to get out of there and back to work. They kept me in for a whole week. I was deeply depressed and didn't know what to do. Then again, when I hit rock bottom, something unexpected happened."

To back up a little: in its negotiations with McEachern, one of their largest clients was represented by a man we will call Mr. Patella. Milan knew that McEachern would have a hard time fulfilling that contract without him, so just before he left the firm, he made a private call to Mr. Patella and told him if at any time in the future he ran into trouble, to give him a ring. In the hospital, when Milan was going through his worst depression, the telephone beside his bed rang. "The man on the other end didn't introduce himself but simply said, 'Are you ready?' 'Mr. Patella,' I said, without hesitation, 'you have no idea what you've just done. You have saved me from suicide.' That call restored my self-confidence. Ron Macari was not only intimately familiar with the contract but was eager to prove I could depend on him. So that was how ucs began to provide cleaning services to one of Canada's largest retailers."

Two Lessons

LESSON ONE: FACE DIFFICULT SITUATIONS HEAD ON

ONE REASON FOR Milan's success has been his keen attention to the world around him coupled with his ability to file away information that would one day be useful to him. During his time at McEachern, Milan learned from Joe Grguric how to deal with disgruntled employees and how to deal with people in general. One day, a young cleaner came into Joe and Milan's office, tossed his keys on the desk, and somewhat rudely gave them an ultimatum: if they didn't pay him more, they could do the cleaning themselves. At that time, Milan still believed that in situations when you don't know how to proceed, it's appropriate to buy time by prevaricating, so, naturally, he was curious to see how Joe would handle this young man's demand.

Joe pulled open a drawer in his desk, rummaged around in it for a while, closed it, pulled open another one, and then, with icy calm, said, "You know, I'm looking for more money, but I can't seem to find any." I looked at the young man out of the corner of my eye, and I thought, "So that's it, he's going to quit."

The young man looked at Joe and said, "All right, I'm on my way." He got up, turned on his heel, and walked out. Joe shouted after him, "Does that mean you're going back to work?"

"Of course," the young man replied, and disappeared through the door. That incident taught me a rare lesson. Joe could have lied, could have tried to persuade him to stay, could have made excuses. He might even have made vague promises of a future raise, and then have the young man showing up in his office every week. By using the direct approach, he sorted out the situation in a couple of minutes, gained his respect, and saved the company the expense of looking for a new employee.

LESSON TWO: ALWAYS KEEP YOUR WORD

During his time as a national manager with McEachern, Milan made a lot of acquaintances, among them Pat Carson. Pat once approached Milan with the suggestion he create a new line of cleaning products. This interested Milan, and at his own expense, he developed a proposal. When he took it to Carson for his approval, he found a young man in his office whom Pat introduced as "your new partner." That was news to Milan. There had been no talk before of a partner. He replied that he didn't need a partner. They argued back and forth for a while but didn't come to a solution. Finally, Milan stood up, tossed his proposal on Pat's desk, and walked out, saying over his shoulder, "It's all yours. I'm out of here." In the doorway, he turned and added,

"By the way, it cost me $8,000 to do this. Who's going to pay me?" He noted Carson's reaction: "Don't worry," Pat shot back. "I'll settle up with you." Milan turned on his heel and walked out.

They didn't speak again for almost two years. One day, the telephone in Milan's office rang. It was Pat Carson. "Look, I've just heard about a unique offer," Carson said. "The bank is selling prestigious two-acre lots right next to a golf club in Nobleton. It would be a great buy, and you could make a decent profit on it because it's a bankruptcy sale. I'll go with you, and I'll help you choose something that will certainly pay off."

Milan, Kathy, and Pat Carson.

Shortly after that they went to the site:

There was one beautiful lot that appealed to me, and I decided to buy it for $50,000. My plans were to build a grand family house on it, but then I had second thoughts. I had no interest in proving anything to anyone. Within the year, I sold the lot for $135,000. And thus, the eight grand that Pat "owed" me was paid back. But even more than the profit, I valued his honourable behaviour.

When the agent who sold my lot handed me the cheque, he asked me what I was going to do with the money. I had originally thought of investing it in my company, but his question got me thinking: "You know, I was born in a mill in a village back home and I've always wanted to have a farm, but it can't be just any old farm!"

"As a matter of fact," the agent said, "I just happen to have a nice farm for sale. Tell me what you're looking for."

"My farm has to have a lot of room, about 250 acres."

The agent nodded.

"There has to be a river running through it."

The agent nodded.

"And all the buildings should be old, so I can tear them down and build new ones."

The agent stood up. "I think we should go and take a look!"

The farm cost exactly $135,000, and it seemed to me that it was meant for me. This was in 1982. By now, we had three children and were still living in a little bungalow in Burlington.

Kathy, Mother, Milena

THE 1970s WERE A demanding time for Milan. He worked long hours, driven more by his own creative energy than by the promise of wealth. Then, in 1978, two things happened that brought Milan great happiness. That year, his mother came to Canada for the first time. The Communist regime had begun to allow its citizens to visit relatives abroad, and from then on, she came to visit every year.

As for his father, shortly after Milan's departure from Czechoslovakia, he had been sentenced to another five years in prison — ostensibly for "illegal enterprise" but also, probably, as punishment for Milan's "betrayal" in leaving the country. They had also sentenced Milan, in absentia, to two years for the "crime" of not returning from a trip abroad. As a result, his father came to Canada only twice, once in 1979 and once in 1982. By that time, he was battling the cancer he'd

Milan's father on a visit to Canada in 1979, with his grandchildren Robert, Michael, and baby Kathy.

brought home from Jáchymov prison, where he had worked in a uranium mine. He was proud of his son's success and let him know it in subtle ways, though in keeping with his characteristic reticence, he never praised him.

The event that brought Milan and Milena the greatest joy was the birth of their daughter, Kathy. It was something that almost didn't happen.

In those days, Milan spent most of his time — when he was at home — with his two sons, Robert and Michael. Mostly, he played soccer with them. Robert wasn't that keen, but Michael was good at it and enjoyed it.

One fall morning in 1977, Milena confided to Milan that she was pregnant again. Milan was not very happy about this; first, because it took him by surprise (Milena was using birth control), and second, because they had already decided not to have any more children. In their current situation, Milan felt they couldn't afford another child. The fact is, however, he'd always longed to have a daughter and may have felt some disappointment that fate had given them only boys. But at that moment, his practical instincts prevailed, and he was blunt and unsentimental about it: "I'm sorry, but you're going to have to make it go away."

He remembers Milena's reaction vividly: "She looked at me in horror. Birth control was one thing, but an abortion was an entirely different matter. I don't think I really appreciated what an abortion means for a woman. She begged and pleaded, but I was adamant. Finally, she was so worn down by arguing that her insistence weakened, and I began to feel she'd eventually give in. We both fell asleep utterly exhausted."

That night, Milan had a dream:

I'm walking across a beautiful mountain pasture covered in flowers and green grass. A large herd of cows is grazing in the pasture. There is a white wooden fence across the pasture and, in the middle, a gate with a pointed archway over it. In front of the gate, there's a beautiful little girl, about five years old. I approach her and give her a wink. The little girl winks back at me. I am charmed by this innocent game. At that moment, I hear the thundering of hooves. The herd of cows is rushing straight at us. Without thinking, I sweep the little girl into my arms and throw her on my back to protect her from the stampeding herd. I seem to have magic powers, because I'm able to bring the stampeding herd to a halt with a wave of my hand.

To this day, it still seems as fresh to me as if I'd dreamed it yesterday. I can still feel the cows' skin on the palm of my free hand as I'm pushing them away so they won't harm the little girl. At that moment, I woke up and shook Milena awake. "Don't worry," I said. "You don't have to give up the child. It's going to be a little girl, and we're going to keep her." Milena was greatly relieved, and I began to tell all our friends that we were expecting a girl. (At that time, it wasn't common to analyze the amniotic fluid to determine the sex of a child.) I was 100 percent sure that the little girl in my dream was our future daughter. I wanted our friends to understand that there are higher powers over which we have no control.

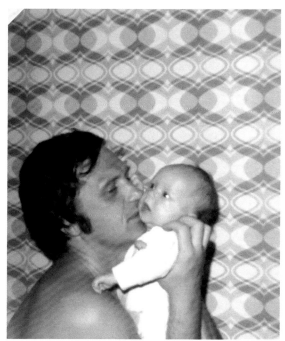

Milena's pregnancy went by without complications. On June 28, 1978, at 5 AM, when the doctor called to tell me I had a beautiful daughter, I replied, "I know, doctor." He probably thought I was slightly mad, but I was more certain that we were going to have a girl than I was of our company's future success. When I picked up both my girls from the hospital I was in heaven. Coming home with Kathy was a beautiful experience for Milena. There were no bedbugs, no smoke from burnt eggs, just our own comfortable home. She didn't sit on the edge of the bed and cry. She glowed with the pride and the joy of an experienced mother. Even so, it never occurred to me to buy her flowers.

ABOVE

Milan with his father and mother on a visit to Canada, outside the Norseman Street offices, 1982.

RIGHT

Milan's mother, aged fifty-five, in 1968.

Perhaps all this had something to do with Milan's mother's spiritualism and those seances in the mill, when Milan's father was in jail, and with the prophecies of the fortune-teller. In 1979, the year both Milan's parents came to Canada, a very special relationship developed between Milan's mother and their new daughter. Even though Kathy never learned Czech (Robert is the only one of Milan and Milena's children who speaks Czech), the two of them grew very close over the years. No one was more delighted about this than Milan. "Love does not need words," he says.

> My mother was very affectionate, and she would often take her granddaughter in her arms and cuddle her. In that way, she created a lifelong bond. Kathy seriously claims that since her grandmother's death, she speaks to her in spirit. I have no doubt that that's true. Kathy has a spirit that can reach beyond the limits of life and death. If she was able to appear to me in a dream before she was born, I have no doubt that she can communicate in spirit with her grandmother. It has certainly had a huge influence on her own motherhood. Sometimes when I watch her cuddle her son — my grandson, Cameron — I remember those times she spent with my mother long ago. I'm immensely grateful to fate for providing moments like this, despite all the separations and hardships.

Milan's own bond with his mother is no less powerful. "My mother is with me always," he says. "I still feel her beside me. And I still haven't gotten over her death. I suppose I will feel that way until I die. And then we will meet somewhere on the way into the unknown."

28

Farmer

MILAN BELIEVES THAT apart from natural catastrophes, there isn't much he can't handle, including war, political upheavals, and death. Certainly, he successfully solved all of his entrepreneurial challenges, and when he'd made enough to buy the farm of his dreams, his attitude, in the tradition of the hero of *In the Glow of Millions,* was: "I'm a country boy, so why shouldn't I be able to master farming as a profitable hobby?"

So, after buying three horses, which provided his family with a lot of fun, he decided to raise pigs. The farm was big enough, and a neighbouring family, who lived in one of the buildings on the property, agreed to help look after them. Agriculture (or at least raising pigs) was a very different kind of activity from running a cleaning business. It was supposed to be a hobby, but in Milan's mind, hobbies

FACING

The Kroupas' farmhouse, 2001.

175

should also make money. For Milan, an entrepreneurial hobby that became a losing proposition would quickly cease to be a hobby and become a liability.

Milan began by buying a hundred piglets. One was earmarked for a real Czech pig-slaughtering ceremony in the Kroupa household; the rest were meant to be sold to hungry customers. But things didn't turn out to Milan's satisfaction. The family records do not indicate what kind of domestic pig-slaughtering festival it was, but it was probably successful, because the records do show the piglet in question had been properly fattened. But when Milan sold the rest of the pigs and did the math, he found he'd lost money. At that moment, he made an executive decision: "We're not going to raise pigs anymore!" And he went out and bought twenty-five male calves.

"I could see them in my imagination, grazing peacefully on my 250 acres. It was a vision from the old film about the Argentinean rancher that I'd seen when I was twelve."

But young calves and dreaming aren't always a good fit: "Young bulls are fighters, and they don't get along with each other. So I had to have them gelded and turn them into steers."

During one operation, the vet cut into a calf's urinary tract and its urine began to flow into its stomach, causing it to swell up very badly. In the end, it had to be euthanized and its meat sold for dog food. The rest of the herd did well, however, grazing in the sunshine on the succulent grass and gaining weight. At the end of the season, trailers came and carried the steers off to market. Again, Milan did the math, only to discover he hadn't made a penny.

"I realized that for the farm to make money I would have to produce my own feed, because good-quality feed was expensive. So I got the idea of growing my own feed and selling whatever was left."

The problem was that although he was a country boy, he didn't know much about hay. He was also unprepared for how much hard work was involved. During the haying season, when he came home to the farm after a week's work in the city, what awaited him was not recreation but the drying and the turning of hay. As long as the weather was good, he could handle it. The problems began when it rained during the week, and it also didn't help that he had no experience in drying hay. When he stuck his hand into a pile of hay, it seemed dry to him, so he gave the order to have the hay baled.

"That was my favourite job, because it had real meaning," Milan says. "I had all the equipment I needed, and I loved the drama of the machines as they bound the hay into bales, which were carried along a conveyor belt and up into the wagons. When the square bales were sent up into the new floor I had built for them in the barn, I was in seventh heaven."

His sojourn in seventh heaven didn't last long. The next time he came to the farm, he noticed wisps of smoke seeping out of the hay in the loft.

"I immediately called a neighbour, who came over with a quantity of salt. We separated the bales and then put salt on them. We managed to save the hay, but at the same time, we ruined it as animal feed. It was even worse with the bales that were left at the bottom of the wagon. Smoke was already pouring out, and when we dragged them outside they burst into flames before our eyes. That moment chilled me. I realized that we had barely managed to fend off a catastrophe. It was the end of my romance with hay."

It was not, however, the end of Milan's dream of farming. Anyone who knows Milan would have expected nothing less. This man, who embodied the tradition of a father whom not even Communist prisons could dissuade from doing business, who had been inspired by *In the*

Milan and his mother
at the farm.

Milan presides over
an old-fashioned
Czech-style pig roast.

Glow of Millions, and moreover, who seemed, in his life, to echo the Churchillian challenge, "We shall never surrender!" would not be so easily put off. So he bought thirty hens.

The experiment began well. The hens laid eggs. Milan's family enjoyed eating them, and Milena and Milan's mother outdid themselves baking cakes. Milan even made an agreement with Sláva Duriš, who owned a Tim Hortons coffee shop, to provide him with fresh eggs in exchange for day-old doughnuts, which Milan then fed to the chickens. It was an ideal situation, but unfortunately it didn't last very long.

"One day, I noticed that the chickens were laying fewer and fewer eggs, and I thought someone must be stealing them. I asked my mother's advice." His mother, an experienced farmer, stuck her fingers into the hens' vents, concluded their laying days were over, and told Milan they'd have to be sold for meat. "I didn't want to do that," Milan says, "but I reluctantly agreed. 'All right, Mum, go ahead and kill them.' 'Not on your life!' my mother replied. 'I'll scald them, and pluck them, and eviscerate them, but you have to kill them yourself.' I saw that there was no way I could get her to change her mind. So I said to myself, 'You're a man, are you not?'"

Milan got himself a machete and a decent chopping block, then went around the yard, rehearsing what he was about to do. Finally, he caught a chicken, laid it on the block, chopped its head off, and quickly let go of its body in disgust. Then something strange happened.

"I finally understood where the famous saying 'to run around like a chicken with its head chopped off' came from. The hen ran around the yard until it bled to death. In the end, I felt like the Lord High Executioner. I executed all thirty chickens, plus the rooster, which in any case got on our nerves with its crowing, and I took them all to my mother. Mother already had a big vat full of boiling water ready, and for a long time after that we had a lot of wonderful soup and many good meals."

The Midas Touch

MILAN'S MIDAS TOUCH does not appear to be as universal as Midas's was. Clearly, he didn't manage to change fast food or farm produce into gold. But otherwise, almost everything he touched turned into dollars. The building lot in Nobleton was typical. It began with a plan to create a new line of cleaning products, which never happened, but it led him, through Pat Carson, to the property near the golf course in Nobleton that he bought for $50,000 and sold a year later for $135,000.

Another example is the series of transactions with his operational buildings in Toronto. One day, towards the end of the 1970s, Milan was sitting in his office on Munster Avenue, when a real estate agent named Collier, who specialized in commercial buildings, came to see him. He mentioned that not far from Milan's office he was selling a building for

FACING

Milan and his first Mercedes, 1982.

181

a price that seemed pretty decent. Milan's current building was getting too small for the expanding business, and he saw Collier's suggestion as a nudge from fate that he should sell and buy something bigger. He had bought the building for $250,000, and he suggested to Collier that he put it on the market for $350,000. Collier thought the building was still only worth about $250,000, but Milan stood his ground. So did Collier, but in the end, though disapprovingly, he listed Milan's building for $350,000. As fate would have it, Milan was right: within two weeks, he got an offer for $340,000.

The purchase agreement stated the sale had to close in three months, which gave Milan only that long to find a new building. Once again, as in a fairy tale, Collier showed up in his office. He knew about a good buy on Paxman Street, not far from Milan's current address. The building was eleven thousand square feet, almost double the size of his current building; the interior was in need of repair, and the owner was asking $525,000.

"I went to check it out, and when I examined the breaker box I saw, to my astonishment, that a quality control tag hanging on the wall had been put there by my former employer, which meant that I had probably put it there myself. I thought this was good karma. I was going to receive $320,000 in cash for the sale of my building, so I started to negotiate."

Naturally, before he began negotiating, Milan acquainted himself with any information that might play to his advantage. He discovered the most recent tenant had been a French company that had had a contract to repair Toronto streetcars. It had lost its contract the previous year and moved out. The building had stood empty ever since, and so far, the owner hadn't received a single offer. Owning a building costs money in taxes and basic maintenance, and Milan knew the owner of an empty building would be anxious to get rid of it as quickly as he could.

"I managed to bargain them down to $450,000. Ten years later, when our firm had grown to the point where I had to move into an even larger space, I sold the building on Paxman Street for $1.2 million. I then bought a nice modern building on Hedgedale Road in Brampton, where our Canada-wide offices are to this day."

It's worth mentioning that Milan paid cash for all the buildings, as though mortgages simply didn't exist. That is true both for his real estate holdings, which are separate from his basic cleaning activity, and for his purchase of the former military air base in Edenvale, which we will read about in a subsequent chapter.

Milan's Midas touch also worked beyond real estate. When his attempts to raise pigs, cattle, hens, and hay didn't succeed, and the neighbouring farmer refused to rent his fields because they were waterlogged and unproductive, Milan drained the fields, cleared the property, and combined the smaller fields into one big field. In the end, the neighbouring farmer paid him $9,000 a year for the use of it.

But Milan had a quality that Midas may not have had and that played a significant role in his success: "I think that my greatest strength is my ability to keep calm in crisis situations." He claims to actually enjoy such situations, because they give him the opportunity to solve a problem and create something new and different. "I find it exciting when everyone else around me is panicking, and it's up to me to save the situation. It flatters my ego."

A major crisis erupted in 1997, when Milan's company, which at the time was responsible for cleaning all of a major client's buildings in Canada, lost its Quebec contract and thus a considerable portion of its annual earnings. As a result, doing business in Quebec was no longer profitable, even though Milan still had smaller contracts there, such as Home Depot. His Quebec employees saw the situation as catastrophic, and in his place many entrepreneurs may well have abandoned Quebec altogether. But Milan did not give up.

"I knew we had first-class people in Quebec. The head of operations was a fantastic fellow I could count on 100 percent. I believed that if I gave my managers my word they would not lose their jobs, they would do everything in their power to get new contracts for us. And that's what happened. We signed a contract with the Metro supermarket chain, and that restored our business to the same level we had enjoyed before. Moreover, on the basis of that success, we expanded our activities into the Maritime provinces."

That expansion was largely due to his son Michael, who by this time was engaged in the management of the firm.

Tears Are Shed

IT WAS A LOVE THAT GREW from a chance meeting in the bar called Speciál, across from the Municipal House in Prague. At the time, Milena was eighteen. It was spring, and she and a friend went out in their ball gowns, because they were going to a school prom that evening. They had an hour to spare and dropped in to their favourite bar, where some of their friends were sitting with two boys they did not know. One of them had blue eyes, and he took a long look at Milena and she at him. She couldn't help but notice him, because — as she remembered it later — he looked refined and elegant. She paid even closer attention to him at their next accidental meeting in the same bar, when he made her laugh. Milan had ordered some wieners, and when he began to slice them, a piece flew off the plate and sailed across the bar. That laughter made her heart beat faster, and Milan, for his part, was already head over heels in love with Milena. Even though she knew he was married, she decided to link her destiny to his. Together they planned their escape over the border to the West, and together they would begin their pilgrimage as émigrés when they reunited in Vienna on December 27, 1966.

There were times when they loved each other very deeply. Although she sensed Milan was sometimes involved with other women, and although she knew she did not want an open marriage, she continued to love him. She felt Milan would never abandon her: after all, hadn't he gone all the way back to Prague because of her?

Milan couldn't imagine tolerating it if Milena took a lover, but he saw no problem with having the occasional romantic episodes with other women himself, even though he realized how unfair and one-sided this was. Milan makes no secret of his admiration for women:

What I respect most about women is that they are a pillar of the family. Today, the average woman has at least three jobs: her regular employment, looking after the family, and looking after her husband. Even if they really take care of themselves, and work out in their free time to keep their figure looking good, and — if they can afford it — have cosmetic surgery to please their husbands, many husbands will still seek out a mistress a decade or two younger. He can be overweight and balding, and yet he's the one who thinks he has the right to fall for a twenty-five-year-old chick. That's how it was in our case, the only difference being that I wasn't overweight or balding.

What I regret most is that for most of our life together I took Milena for granted. She longed for fulfillment within our marriage. I didn't give her that fulfillment, and that is my greatest sin. In that sense, I was a shit.

I thought that I was fulfilling my responsibilities as long as I provided for my family. There was a certain male chauvinism in my attitude, of which I am not exactly proud. In the course of my business, various women literally offered themselves to me, and I took it in my stride, as one of the advantages of being a guy. I treated it as a sport and a pleasant diversion in what was otherwise a rat race. One of my involvements was with Joy, a beautiful black woman from Jamaica.

Milan recalled the "prophecy" of his mother's fortune-teller, who many years before had predicted that, in another country, on the other side of the big pond, he would have problems with a woman with dark eyes. Joy indeed had dark eyes and beautiful black hair, and Milan succumbed to her charms. Because she wasn't well off, he once bought furnishings for her entire flat, not so much out of generosity (Milan is one of those rare people who don't feel the need to disguise their motives), but because it made him feel good to be able to afford it, to feel rich and successful. Unfortunately, it wasn't the only feeling their relationship evoked in him.

Joy would occasionally call the office, and Milena would answer the phone. Milan — who is convinced women are endowed with a special instinct that enables them to sense when the man in their life has a romantic interest on the side — began to worry Milena would find out, because although he considered such a dalliance his natural right, he didn't want to risk losing his family. His dilemma became potentially tragic when Joy announced she was pregnant and would not give up the child.

Milan's agricultural experiment had ended with him renting his farm to a neighbouring farmer (the rent more than covered the expenses of running the farm), pulling down the old buildings, and putting up a small house for his family, where they could spend their rare moments of free time. On receiving news about his impending paternity, he went alone to the farm. He lay down in the grass and cried. The following week, he returned there with his family. In the evening, when the children were asleep, he sat down with Milena in the living room.

I sat there and stared silently at the carpet. Milena finally broke the silence. "You've got a problem, haven't you?" I nodded. "You've got somebody pregnant?" I nodded again. "Well, it would be best if you moved out."

Suddenly I felt as though I were back once more on the road through the field when my mother confronted me about Růženka's pregnancy. Even though Milena spoke aloud the words I was most afraid to hear, at that moment a great weight was lifted off my shoulders. It was out in the open, and I felt a sense of relief. I moved to the farm to think things through.

However superficially undramatic his confession to Milena was, what followed was equally undramatic: Milan and Milena did not get a divorce, and Milan continued to provide for Milena as though they were still living together. He fulfilled his financial responsibilities to his last child and to the mother. He devoted a lot of his time to his legitimate children, mainly Michael, who demonstrated a talent for soccer. But he had, and still has, his closest relationship with his daughter, Kathy. Perhaps this is in part because he had initially been against her arrival in the world, until that magical dream persuaded him how wonderful it would be to have the daughter he had always longed for. When he moved out, Kathy wrote him a letter saying how much she missed him, forgiving him for everything and asking him

Family portrait.

LEFT TO RIGHT:
Robert, Kathy, Milan, Milan Jr., Michael.

to come back. The letter reopened a wound that had not yet healed: "I still feel that letter as a dagger to my heart," Milan says. He promised to examine himself more deeply. And he did:

It took years for me to make sense of everything. I believe we store up a lot of information and images in our subconscious, and our subconscious occasionally throws something up into the light of day and it's up to us to learn from that. One day, I was watching a National Geographic program on television about the mating dance of a bird of paradise. The male had beautiful feathers, and he twisted and shook himself before a completely ordinary-looking female, spreading his little wings and his elaborate tail, wagging his head and puffing up his chest. After a few minutes of this, the female seemed bored, turned away, and flew off. "You idiot," I said to myself, "that's exactly how you've been behaving."

Often, the rivers of our lives suddenly become calm after a period of turbulence, and that happened to Milan and Milena, who have remained friends.

"We have a lot of wonderful memories," Milan says. "We always spend Christmas and the children's birthdays together. The children are close to me and to their mother but in different ways. They would protect their mother in any crisis, and they come to me when they need help. But who knows, maybe one day their turn will come; I may need their help in my old age."

A Small Miracle
in Edenvale

IF YOU DRIVE NORTH FROM TORONTO at the end of July or
the beginning of August and head west for Wasaga Beach along
Highway 26 towards Stayner, you will drive through countryside
of golden fields of corn, interspersed with greyish-silver strips of
barley and oats. Eventually, you will pass leafy woodlots, and then
suddenly, on one side of the road, the modern world will announce
itself prominently on a large sign: Edenvale Aerodrome. On display
close by is an impressive decommissioned Soviet MiG fighter with
the Czech insignia on its wings and rudder. (Friends of Milan from
Stříbro, whom he brought over to Edenvale, restored the plane to
glorious mint condition.)

Ever since he had watched some men experimenting with a glider
when he was still a young boy, flying had fascinated Milan. In Toronto,

when the opportunity arose, he took flying lessons and even bought a small ultra-light aircraft. When he was practising stalls with his flight instructor in April 2003, what Milan saw from the air was a few hundred acres of wooded land and a large clearing in the middle of which were disused runways overgrown with weeds, grass, and shrubs. His instructor told him it was an old Royal Canadian Air Force aerodrome from the Second World War, where pilots received basic training before being transferred to England to fight against the Luftwaffe. The aerodrome was decommissioned after the war, and all the buildings were torn down. Later, during the Cold War, the Canadian army built a large, fourteen-thousand-square-foot underground bunker on the property, which served as a listening post for intelligence gathering.

The old aerodrome captured Milan's imagination, and he began doing research into its history. He read that in Ottawa, in December 1939, shortly after the British Commonwealth had signed off on a training program, it was decided that every operational aerodrome had to have an auxiliary airfield nearby in case bad weather or other circumstances shut it down. The command centre of the Royal Canadian Air Force at Borden decided it needed two auxiliary aerodromes, and for the first, they chose a parcel of land in Edenvale, consisting of 500 cleared acres and 150 lightly wooded acres with excellent drainage and three gravel pits. By October 1941, the Edenvale auxiliary aerodrome was almost operational, but two months before that, the first aircraft, probably a Harvard T-6 trainer, had already landed there. Edenvale was soon abuzz with these aircraft, and this activity continued throughout the war. When the war was over, and later, when the Cold War ended, the glory of a place through which heroes had passed began to fade, until all that remained were ghostly, mute echoes of those training planes and the overgrown runways.

Milan discovered the abandoned airfield was for sale, and he began to dream. What if he were to buy it for his own use? In his mind, he could already see his own runway and hangar. He even imagined a new residence, a lavish villa set in the picturesque Ontario country-side, on top of the bunker, which formed a small hillock above the level of the runways.

He reckoned the Canadian government would ask about $500,000 for it. To his surprise, they wanted far less, but Milan let them think he considered the asking price unrealistically high and bargained them down. He offered to pay in cash, and they agreed on a selling price of $260,000. Milan didn't have $260,000 in cash, but he had the farm he had bought for $135,000 and had greatly improved. He sold it for $700,000 to the neighbour who was renting it. This left him with enough not only to pay for the airfield but also to begin renovations.

Meanwhile, his business instincts alerted him to the commer-cial potential of his new property, and his dream of having a private airport began to change. He began by repairing the runways. It so hap-pened that at that moment, his nephew, Lad'a, had to leave his job as a machinist for Husky and was able to come to work for Milan on the reconstruction of the airfield. They brought in heavy machinery from the farm and set to work. The first job was clearing the runways of the small trees and bushes that had sprung up. The second was building Milan's personal hangar. And that was how the commercialization of Edenvale began.

As soon as they began building the hangar, pilots started com-ing around, expressing an interest in renting hangar space. Before they could develop the commercial viability of the property, however, they had to gain access to Highway 26. This was blocked by a retire-ment home located on the north side of the property. Milan bought the retirement home, and over the next year he moved the residents to other facilities, thus gaining access to not only the highway but also a building where today, after extensive renovations, there are offices, a flying school, Milan's personal residence (quite modest but Milan is happy with it), and a restaurant, Bistro 26. When the runways were cleared and made operational, interest from pilots wanting to rent hangar space grew.

Milan knew that building hangars and renting them out would finance the revitalization of the airfield, and he was particularly drawn to one group of pilots. "They were older men who had formed a club called the Collingwood Classic Aircraft Foundation, a group of hobbyists who not only collected but also repaired and flew historical aircraft, which they took to various fly-ins and exhibitions. I loved their interest in the romance of old planes and the chance it offered to connect with an old military aerodrome where so many pilots had trained during World War II. I could see that their hobby was an expensive one, and moreover, that it demanded expertise and know-how. In short, I was a big fan of these old fellows."

He supported them not only in words but also in deeds. When a hangar in Collingwood, which had so far been rented to them for free, was sold, he offered to share his own hangar with them. He made a special entrance for them and provided space for five aircraft, leaving one for himself. He asked only one thing in return: they change their name to the Edenvale Classic Aircraft Foundation. He then set about adding more hangars. He planned the smallest for his own flight school, but before plans for this were concluded, the members of the club rented that hangar, and they remain there to this day.

Milan knew next to nothing about the construction of hangars, but that didn't discourage him.

I examined various plans on the Internet and decided on a "T" construction. This kind of construction allows for an economic use of space. At the same time, we put in drainage and laid down new asphalt on the landing strips and the aprons in front of the hangars. The original asphalt had been laid down in 1941, so it was badly in need of an overhaul. But the original underbeds were in excellent shape and very stable. Our newest runway, which is 30 metres wide and 1,300 metres long, turned out to be a real success. We used packed sand brought in from the other side of the property as a foundation. I also installed runway lights so that pilots could land at night. A control tower wasn't necessary. Pilots simply connect to our radio frequency, click six times on a button, and presto: the landing lights come on. It looks like a scene from a Hollywood movie. The runway has been there for several years now, and unlike the highways in southern Ontario, which are filled with potholes each spring, our runways are in good shape, because they are not subject to heavy loading.

The former retirement home was in terrible shape, so I had it gutted and renovated. Thanks to my years of experience in business, I always knew where to save money and where economizing doesn't pay. Both in the re-construction of the buildings and in the construction of the hangars and the runways, I always chose better-quality material, even though it was more expensive, because I didn't want to have to repair them every year. For the time being it's paid off.

As far as the drainage was concerned, I decided it would be cheaper to do it ourselves. What can go wrong in digging ditches? We even thought of creating our own pond that would take drainage water away from the hangars. But it wasn't that simple. Before we managed to bulldoze out the pond area, there was a big storm and we had water right up to the hangars. In the end, I had to hire a professional, who dug the ditches, laid the pipes, and at the same time maintained the right drop so that the water would drain off properly.

The airfield now has six fully rented hangars. Each one brings in between $4,500 and $5,000 a month, and the sale of aviation fuel also provides a decent income, mainly because Milan installed pumps where the pilots could serve themselves using their credit cards. A third source of income comes from an unexpected source — a group of bodyguards, led by a veteran of the Vietnam War, who are trained to protect politicians and other famous people. They liked the area around the bunker. First, they rented the area for a few days, but soon they extended the lease. Milan found their activities amusing: "I watched them in action and it was fascinating. The boys brought in old police

FACING
Edenvale aerodrome from the air, with Highway 26 at the top, the new runway, and six new hangars, 2010.

LEFT
Milan and his grandson, Cameron, with his ultra-light Sky Arrow.

cars and trained for a potential attack on a presidential convoy by terrorists who ambushed the convoy from the small woodlot on the edge of our property. There aren't many places where they could do what they want, even simulate car crashes, but this is one of them."

New clients interested in renting hangar space are always showing up. He made space for three new hangars on his property, each one with room for ten aircraft. As soon as he has contracts with five new customers, he starts building.

Milan never slavishly follows the standard advice often given in how-to books for would-be entrepreneurs, such as "people don't plan to fail, but they often fail to plan," which Milan takes to mean that if you don't plan in detail and draw up a road map to success, you will never reach your goal. Such advice, he thinks, is overrated. He believes leaving the door open to broader possibilities may reveal priceless opportunities. He believes people should enjoy the work they do, learn new things, and remain mentally and emotionally engaged. In Milan's eyes, this gives people a tremendous advantage, especially now that so much work is automated and humans are becoming slaves to artificial intelligence.

He is constantly being reminded of how important it is to leave the door open. A short time ago, Milan was approached by a firm that wanted to develop plans for a field of solar panels on the unused part of the airfield. As well as bringing in new income and giving Milan the opportunity to learn something completely new, the panels will provide twenty-nine megawatts of green electricity to the Ontario power grid.

The Edenvale aerodrome now has hangars to house eighty aircraft. (All of them except two are fully occupied.) The monthly sale of fuel is around 12,000 litres. And then there are the fly-ins for aircraft from all over North America. It has also become a meeting place for classic cars. On August 6, 2011, 125 sports aircraft flew in, and 200 rebuilt historical cars were also on display to 5,000 visitors. This fly-in, like those before it and those that would come after it, was organized by the Edenvale Classic Aircraft Foundation, who were joined by the classic car enthusiasts. As he had done with the earlier events, Milan lent them his airfield. The 2014 event was even more successful: there were 300 sports aircraft (making it the largest fly-in of its kind in Canada), 280 classic cars, and an attendance of 8,000.

32

Bistro 26

WHEN MILAN PURCHASED the retirement home, he was paying not just for the building but also for access to Highway 26. The structure was very run-down and required extensive reconstruction. Milan was particularly taken with the kitchen. He could see that as the number of hangars increased, so would the number of pilots who would be interested in a good cup of coffee, hamburgers, and other kinds of fast food. It was a mere step from the idea to the realization. Milan renovated the entire kitchen and installed a professional pastry oven and other improvements, which cost him more than $200,000. He hired a neighbour who could bake excellent pies, and thus a small coffee shop came into being.

At that time, Milan and his partner, Anna Maria, together with another couple, David Hadfield and his wife, Robin, who were active members of the Edenvale Classic Aircraft Foundation, would often dine at a restaurant called Füd, in the nearby town of Stayner. David is a commercial pilot who flies the Canada–Hong Kong route. (David's older brother, Chris Hadfield, perhaps the most famous astronaut in the world, gave Milan a signed photograph of himself, and Milan is eagerly looking forward to the day when Chris Hadfield will land his plane at the Edenvale airfield.)

Milan was impressed with the restaurant in Stayner, because of both its cuisine and the approach of the owner, Regan Gorman. Before he knew it, Regan had agreed to move his restaurant to the airfield in Edenvale. Milan added a new dining room with a view of the airfield, which is now the main dining area. The agreement was for one year, but this project was one of the few that didn't work out for Milan. Although Regan was able to attract many of his old clientele to Edenvale, it was not enough to pay the rent, and he ended up having to borrow from Milan. At the end of the year, Milan extended Regan's contract for half a year. It still didn't work out. But Milan refused to let go of this star: he settled up with Regan and closed the restaurant, reopening it himself some time later under the name Bistro 26, with his daughter, Kathy, in charge. Today, it is slowly but surely beginning to turn a profit.

Both Milan and Kathy have taken a great deal of care to get it right. They began by surveying their customers, asking them what kind of food they wanted to see on the menu, whether they were satisfied with the service, where they had come from, and how long they stayed. Milan learned customers had begun to come from Barrie, half an hour away, with a population of 140,000, and many motorists stopped in on their way to Collingwood, Wasaga Beach, and Blue Mountain. Recently, Bistro 26 has begun to attract wedding parties and groups who want to celebrate anniversaries and other events in the romantic setting of the airfield. There has also been an increased number of visits from private aircraft owners from airfields as far away as Oshawa, Windsor, and Brampton, who fly in for get-togethers over a good meal. All of this helps spread the reputation and prestige of the Edenvale aerodrome and its restaurant.

Not everything has worked out. Milan has tried twice to establish a flying school, but such a project requires a high number of students and considerable outlays. Nor did he manage to realize an idea he had to build residences around the edge of the airfield for the owners of private planes, who would have, in addition to garages for their cars, a private hangar and direct access to the runways. The project ran into trouble with zoning bylaws that do not permit mixing residential and commercial uses on the same property.

But the benefits of this star are by no means exhausted. Its influence is spreading outwards like ripples from a stone dropped in water. The airfield has become an important economic driver in the fertile but industrially dormant countryside around it. Milan pays a considerable amount of taxes to the township of Clearview, where the airfield is located. In the high season, he employs at least a dozen people, and the fly-ins for small planes and drive-ins for classic cars have spread the reputation of Edenvale across Canada.

The star he first caught sight of when he was practising stalls with his instructor so long ago has never lost its magic for him, even though he has had to give up some of his more elaborate schemes. But even in its more modest form, the airport is a business that gives him a lot of satisfaction. To this day, he loves his airfield with a boyish passion, the same kind of passion with which he loved the mill in Dřetovice. He loves flying, which always gives him an exhilarating sensation of freedom. He loves to feel the controls in his hands and still finds it exciting to fly above the earth and watch the world from above — people going about their business, sowing tomorrow's crops, swimming in the lake, heading for a weekend at the cottage. It reminds him of the days when, as a goaltender, he had the opportunity to size up the competing team from a distance. This view from above makes it possible to see the world from a different perspective. And he still enjoys practising stalls, because it reminds him of the moment the seeds of a dream were sown.

The aerodrome has another level of meaning for Milan: the bunker on which he once planned to build his mansion could well have played an important role during the Cold War, when Milan's native land and all of Eastern Europe were a part of the Soviet empire, a time when his father went through the hell of prison and Milan had to fend for himself. (The MiG at the entrance is also a reminder of that time.) When he first stepped into the vast underground space, he felt he was entering a place steeped in the atmosphere of the Cold War. It was one of those outposts that were meant to help defend the most precious thing man has fought for over the centuries, freedom.

Today, the financial backing of his firm, United Cleaning Services, allows Milan to "play." But, as always, Milan sees no reason why his "playing" should not pay for itself, as well as produce a healthy profit. In this case, he has proven that even a modest corner of rural Ontario can be very lucrative. In short, where there was once nothing more than ruined, weed-infested runways, Milan created a place pulsing with life and hope.

Although nothing is guaranteed, Milan has a few good years ahead of him, and he will certainly reach for a few more stars. This may happen on his aerodrome, where he is now in the process of renovating the bunker. But even if he never did anything else again, what he has managed to accomplish on this once derelict piece of land, and what he has done by building his company, United Cleaning Services, surely brings him much satisfaction.

New Theories about the Origin of the World and Other Interesting Things

THE EUROPE INTO WHICH Milan was born was in the throes of the greatest military conflict in history. When that war ended, Europe settled into an uneasy peace, particularly in the countries of Central and Eastern Europe, where the victors turned the government and the lives, the property, and the souls of their citizens over to Stalin. Terror simply shed its Nazi uniform, donned a Soviet uniform, and continued to rule for the next forty years. The Soviet regimes drove millions of people out of their homes. Milan Kroupa was one of those. Now his native land, just like its neighbours, is trying to recover its soul, while the leaders of the nations that have clashed for millennia try to forge a new and united Europe.

In Milan's lifetime, the flames of war have flared up in different places all around the world. In the 1960s, humanity escaped nuclear catastrophe by a hair when Khrushchev sent ships loaded with nuclear warheads to Cuba. Over the years, Africa has seen its share of carnage. Conflicts in the Middle East are still raging; the horrors of war are daily occurrences in Syria and Iraq. So far, no one can predict how Europe will come to terms with the influx of millions of refugees, or how it will deal with renewed threats from Russia. There have been huge changes as well in the largest Communist country in the world — China — where the sacred doctrine of collective ownership has been replaced by a system of private enterprise that, however, still remains under the strict control of the Communist Party. All that is left of the dream of a world dominated by the Communist International are two small countries: North Korea and Cuba, and even Cuba is beginning to change.

On a cultural level, there have been vast shifts in the way people live. Fifty or sixty years ago, a woman was an anomaly in the so-called male professions, including law; today, women can even be in the majority in such fields. Progress has been made in race relations in the United States. Throughout the planet, more than 500 million people who were once wretchedly poor can now at least live with a little dignity. And hundreds of millions of people, and dozens of countries (some of them for the first time in history) are now included in the category of free countries.

There have also been unbelievable advances in technology. On the one hand, who in 1942 could have imagined you could write something on a screen, click on a virtual button, and send your immortal words instantaneously to the screen of a correspondent anywhere in the world? On the other hand, who could have imagined the abuse of this technology might also drive a young woman to commit suicide?

Meteorologists have warned us that by polluting the atmosphere of our planet we are causing the melting of the ice caps and the rising of sea levels, which will cause the catastrophic flooding of a considerable part of the planet if nothing is done to prevent it. From the laboratories of physicians, mathematicians, and astronomers came the news, based on data provided by the Hubble telescope, that they had finally discovered how the universe might have come into being. Now called the Big Bang theory, it is said to have occurred quite simply: in a single instant, and in a single spot, a huge explosion gave rise to all the starry constellations, scattering them outward into an ever-expanding universe.

In 1942, almost no one could have imagined doctors would one day be able to replace your hip, your lungs, your heart, or — as Milan experienced seven months after celebrating his seventy-first birthday — your knee. And finally, in Milan's seventy-third year, not only can you buy beer in Toronto on a Sunday, you can even buy Czech beer, including Pilsner, on tap. What was once a puritanical city with an Anglo-Saxon majority has grown into a cosmopolitan metropolis, the GTA, with around 5 million inhabitants, the third largest urban area in North America. It is said that every ethnic group in the world has a restaurant in Toronto. The majority of the population is no longer Anglo-Saxon, or even Caucasian. Each year, the population increases by about 125,000 people, all of them looking for freedom, dignity, work, wealth, and happiness in the country that Milan still sees as the promised land. As he says, "Canada is the only woman I've ever remained faithful to."

Looking Back: Was It Worth It?

MILAN HAS MANY REASONS to feel satisfied with his life. He has made few decisions he would change. He has never regretted his decision to emigrate. To this day, he remains grateful to his father for having confidence in him, and for preparing him for a life abroad and a life in business, and doing so without regard for his own freedom.

When he flew from Austria to Canada, Milan already had a family, and without really being aware of it — since it was something he inherited from his culture — looking after his family became his main goal. To this day, the fact that he has been able to provide handsomely for his children gives Milan his greatest satisfaction. Most of all, he is proud not just of providing them with material benefits but also of enabling them to look after themselves. All of his sons had to start at the bottom, cleaning as rank-and-file employees of United Cleaning Services.

FACING

Ladislav and Milan with their mother at the mill in Dřetovice in 1990, just after the fall of Communism.

They had to work their way up by their own efforts, climbing the ladder like all the other employees. Today, Michael is the CEO of United Cleaning Services, Robert is in charge of training and safety, and Milan Jr. is the company troubleshooter. Kathy is going into the legal profession. If his feeling of satisfaction is clouded by anything, it is the knowledge that his father, who inspired him not only with dreams of wealth but also with his own example and philosophy of life, was prevented by the Communist regime from enjoying a similar satisfaction. At the same time, it fills him with pride to know his father's spirit was never subdued by that evil ideology, nor could it crush his father's faith in Milan's future success.

Milan has a clear-eyed view of the changes his company has gone through. At the beginning, he had a personal relationship with each of his employees; he was accessible to all of them, all the time. He remembers it as a time when he knew his employees were proud to work for United Cleaning Services. That relationship began to change as the firm grew, and today his employees are beholden to the firm mainly because of the benefits and salaries it provides. Milan, of course, understands this, but he also knows how important it is, both for the employees and for the firm, that everyone knows he or she has the chance to get ahead. That requires the instruction and training of employees, and it demands their commitment to the instruction manuals, which Milan's son Robert has had translated into French and other languages so that new arrivals may more easily fit in.

Milan's relationship with Milena is quite unusual — a relationship that caught fire at a chance meeting in a Prague café and ended with Milena's prosaic final announcement, many years and three children later: "Well, it would be best if you moved out." Milan has always acknowledged the part Milena played in his success and her contribution in raising their children. Moreover, they have remained financial partners: "For every dollar that I take for myself, she gets the same," he says.

But he also knows their breakup was probably unavoidable. They have very different interests. "Milena was always a wonderfully practical woman, but she never expressed any interest in spiritual matters," Milan says. "Such interests, however, increased in me as I grew older. The bond that holds us together now is the children and the grandchildren."

Milan's relationship to the Czech community in Toronto has gone through a number of changes. When he played soccer for Sparta Toronto, Milan and Milena had many Czech acquaintances. "For the first five to seven years, we spoke Czech at home," he says. "But when Milena's English began to improve, the children would come home from school and speak English exclusively, and English gradually became the dominant household language. For a long time, when Milena and I were alone, we spoke Czech, but now we switch languages depending on how we're feeling at the time. But the children all grew up as English-speaking Canadians." Robert still speaks pretty decent Czech; Milan Jr. understands but has a harder time speaking; Kathy only knows a few words.

In the 1990s, the family began to support the Czech-language television program *Nova Vize* (New Vision). The director of the show, Marketa Slepčíková, made a documentary about Milan called *Portrait of a Successful Entrepreneur* and included it in her film *Three Waves of Czechoslovak Emigration,* which she made for the multicultural television station OMNI. Milan is now a regular supporter of *Nova Vize,* the only program broadcasting to the world in Czech outside the Czech Republic.

One event in the Czech community gave him a lot of pleasure: an outing to the Edenvale aerodrome by a group from Sokol — a Czech patriotic society — and their children. The parents provided a picnic for the children, and they bought some of the children an hour's flight in an ultra-light aircraft. Unfortunately, Edenvale is a little too far away from Toronto, where the most populous Czech and Slovak émigré community lives, for regular events like that.

Milan's relationship with one of the largest Czechoslovak community organizations, the Masaryk Institute, now located in the Toronto suburb of Scarborough, was more complicated, mainly because the people around the institute had differing visions for the future of the beautiful park the institute owns. Milan's support was limited to the "loan" of his accountant, who to this day looks after the books of the institute, free of charge.

Along with his fellow exiles, Milan welcomed the fall of the Communist regime in 1989 with unabashed delight. His childhood memories of September 1948, when Communist agents came to arrest his father, added a special quality to his euphoria. At the time — and in the years that followed — it had seemed that the resistance offered by people like Milan's father had no hope of prevailing over an empire that ruled half of two continents. Yet in Czechoslovakia, during the Velvet Revolution, that empire faded away without a single shot being fired. It provided much satisfaction to millions of survivors, who saw they had not made their sacrifices in vain. And the memory of his father was certainly one of the reasons why, in 2009, Milan made the Edenvale aerodrome available for an event called Let Freedom Ring, to mark the forty-first anniversary of the occupation of Czechoslovakia by the armies of the Warsaw Pact. The event, which Milan also sponsored, was organized by the Open Book Group, which is supporting an initiative to erect a monument in Ottawa to the victims of Communism. It was both a cultural and a political event, the kind that under the Communist regime would never have been allowed, something that would have seemed almost incomprehensible to the Canadian guests present.

In 2013, Milan's memories of not being allowed to continue his studies at the Slaný grammar school, nor even at the mill workers' industrial school, influenced his decision to make a generous donation to the program of Czech (and Czechoslovak) studies at the University of Toronto. As an entrepreneur in a country where almost all nationalities in the world mingle, along with their languages and philosophies of life, Milan knows how valuable a knowledge of languages and a broad outlook on the world can be.

Whenever he goes down memory lane and visits his native country, he catches a glimpse of himself sitting in the Tupolev jet, hearing the roar of its engines, and he experiences once again the intense anticipation of finally being free. "I remember I was thinking that everything was okay, and then the stewardess asked us to leave the plane because there was a problem. My heart was in my mouth. I saw myself sitting in Pankrác prison, where my father once spent time. To this day, whenever I fly out of the Prague airport, I break out in a cold sweat."

How I See Milan Kroupa

I **FIRST MET MILAN KROUPA** several years ago, sometime in 2007. I was sitting in the middle of one of Toronto's concert halls, in the second seat from the aisle. Smetana's patriotic tone-poem to Bohemia, "My Homeland," was on the program. As we waited for the concert to begin, the general consul of the Czech Republic in Toronto at the time, Richard Krpáč, stopped by with a tall good-looking man who introduced himself as Milan Kroupa. Milan and I began talking, and before the concert began, we were on a first-name basis and had discovered we'd attended the same grammar school in Slaný, the only differences being that I graduated a year before he was born, and the Communists had only allowed him to go as far as grade ten. I also learned this was the first classical music concert he had ever attended in Canada. That impressed me. In a similar situation, most people would either pretend they went to concerts all the time (most Czechs have rich cultural interests and pretensions), or they simply wouldn't bring it up at all. Milan reacted differently, and his reaction indicated to me that I was in the company of an independent spirit — a man who does not need the crutch of pretence to feel at home in the world. His strength lay in his confidence in himself and in his self-awareness.

FACING

The mill in Dřetovice, 1990.

215

In his childhood and youth, that strength manifested as obstinacy and rebelliousness. Milan had running battles with his main idol, his father. He had skirmishes with his teachers at grammar school, which came to a head when his Czech teacher slapped Milan's face in front of the whole class. His battles with the world continued in the factory where he learned how to operate a lathe, and where he was constantly getting into arguments with his superiors. Had he not been an outstanding soccer player, and had the "comrades" in charge not prided themselves on their soccer teams, he would almost certainly have eventually ended up in prison like his father.

Particularly in his younger years, Milan was not exactly modest, and he always felt the need to stand out. He was aware of his physical attractiveness and his not entirely ordinary abilities, even though, with the exception of girls and soccer, he had no particular interest in cultivating them. In his early youth, he was not averse to lying to get what he wanted. "When I was young, it was very easy for me to get out of sticky situations by lying," Milan admits. "But as I grew older those lies turned bitter in my mouth. It was not just the fear that I might be exposed, but the long and short of it is, I came to feel that lying was beneath my dignity." He is proud of his successes but even prouder of the fact that he achieved them honourably. "My word and my handshake are more valuable than any contract," he says. "This is a hard thing to do in business, because lying and stealing is common in the 'jungle,' as my father saw it. To know how to navigate that jungle without getting hurt, and not become a wild animal yourself, is one of the hardest tests in life."

Milan's need to excel had an impact on his great love, the woman who, even though they now live separately, is still his wife. He was always an independent operator, and independent operators are probably not the most ideal partners in marriage. What they need is the greatest possible freedom to run their lives in their own way. If they are men with a powerful libido, and if they are young, and in their father's absence they are exposed to influences like Milan's Uncle Eda, who enthralled Milan and his brother with stories of his sexual conquests, their path to the garden of marital fidelity is bound to be thorny. Milan was not ideally equipped for a long and faithful marriage, but there were also problems on the side of Milena and her family. Even though there can be no doubt Milena loved Milan, her socially well-placed family had at first looked down on a country boy of limited education whose father was a political prisoner. Milan felt this and was too proud to ignore it. What is remarkable in this case is that Milan continues to share with Milena the phenomenal fruits of his labours.

Did success in Canada spoil the boy from the mill in Dřetovice? I would say the answer is no. Success satisfied his ambition and confirmed his sense of self-worth, but he feels no need to be arrogant about it. Not that he would disparage the beneficent power of his millions. On the contrary, he knows what advantages those millions give him in his everyday life. He is aware of their power far more than people who did not have to fight for their wealth.

His millions have also allowed him to contribute, via United Cleaning Services, to charities such as the Hospital for Sick Children in Toronto and to cancer research. I have already mentioned his support for a program of Czech studies at the University of Toronto and other activities that, without his help, might easily have foundered. Without those millions, he would probably never have dared to buy and revitalize the Edenvale aerodrome and, in doing so, save a piece of Canadian history and create a considerable financial and cultural asset in the Edenvale area. But ultimately, the most important thing for Milan is that he has provided wealth and comfort for his family.

Possessing millions brings other minor benefits as well, including invitations to social events to which ordinary mortals are not invited, such as on one occasion an exclusive pheasant hunt. The hunt was a success, nobody shot anyone else, and the dinner was certainly worth it, if only because Milan sat beside George Eaton, whose family was once one of the richest and most famous in Canada. They owned a chain of prestigious department stores across Canada and built the famous Eaton Centre in the middle of Toronto. However, the firm went bankrupt and the family managed to squander its unbelievable wealth. Milan and George, its youngest scion, talked until 3 AM.

This conversation confirmed what Milan already knew: "An entrepreneur who gains his wealth through his wits, his moral strength, and his hard work has a different relationship to money than his children, who were simply born into it." In Milan's judgement, the Eatons' sense of entitlement undermined their ability to adapt to the demands of the time, and the competition eventually flattened them. For that reason, he is trying to make sure Michael, who is now CEO of United Cleaning, has a sensitive and dynamic style of leadership and is capable of creatively combining tradition, risk, instinct, and the ability to look into the future. "It is important," Milan says, "to see, not just what is, but also what might be. Like my father, who saw not just a pile of scrap wood but also handles for brushes, which could be transported across the channel and sold in England."

Milan knows how much he owes his success to his parents — but also to luck. He knows that so much of his achievement resulted from blindly groping in the dark. But he also knows that a large role has been played by his ability to grasp the star of opportunity and hang onto it. He knows as well that nothing can take the place of the satisfaction he gets from having built, from almost nothing, a company that provides a positive workplace and ongoing opportunities to excel for thousands of people.

Milan still feels himself to be a Czech in the depths of his soul. He thought about doing business in the post-Communist Czech Republic, but their methods are too different from his own. For the Czech Republic to compete successfully in the world, in Milan's view, it would have to automate its production processes:

> In Bohemia they still practise individual production processes, which, of course, produce goods of high quality, because the worker has a personal relationship to the product, but it is also slow and, therefore, expensive. They don't stand a chance against China. They need to be outstanding in something. They also have a long way to go in marketing and advertising before they catch up with the West. Moreover, their approach to business financing is very inflexible. Most of the firms that I looked at as potential business opportunities were not open to accepting loans. They want to pay for everything up front, and in doing so they sabotage their opportunities.

The death of his parents was painful for him. It closed the door to the strongest ties he had with his native country. Even the flour mill, which he saw as his birthright until the Communists confiscated it, doesn't attract him any more. Milan's brother now lives there and has made many changes to it. All that remain are echoes of his childhood.

Milan is not one to hide anything about himself, neither the wildness of his youth, nor his infrequent failures. He is just as open about his relationship to the world around us. His theory about human life is inspired by the zodiac. According to Milan's theory, human souls are reincarnated twelve times, each one under a different sign of the zodiac. In each reincarnation, they learn something new. The final reincarnation is in the sign of the fish, Pisces, Milan and Michael's sign. After that, no one returns to earth and thus will never again have the opportunity to put things right. This belief has awakened in Milan a need to behave honourably and with dignity, not to lie and not to cheat, even though that may offer an opportunity to make a quick profit. In this he differs a great deal from the "hero" of the book *In the Glow of Millions*.

Like the rest of us, he doesn't know where the human soul goes after death. "Our life on earth is limited by our senses, which do not allow us to see, hear, or touch 'God,'" he says. "Officially I don't believe in God, but I can't deny the possibility that there exist spiritual forces which I feel not only in myself, but in my parents. Therefore I hope that when my spirit departs from my body it will continue somewhere up there in the universe, or that it will join forces with other energies that exist on the earth … forces that we, with our limited perceptions, are incapable of detecting."

The assessment of Milan's personality I made at our first encounter has remained with me. Milan has no need of lies or pretence to make an impression, and virtue in such a man lies in his self-knowledge. He has travelled far in his spiritual journey. The centre of his personality is not his millions — as useful as they are — but his heart and soul. I think that one of the final images that will appear to my consciousness when my own soul sets out into the unknown will be Milan, sitting on his ATV, at a safe distance from his runway, beguiling the ozone with the fragrant smoke from his cigar, gazing towards the night sky and wondering in which constellation he will encounter the spirit of his beloved mother.

ACKNOWLEDGEMENTS

First of all, my thanks to Milan Kroupa for his willingness to allow me to take a close look at his life, his family, and his various enterprises. He gave me access to his personal papers, which, along with several conversations with him, were the main source material for this book. It was a pleasure and adventure to be allowed to get lost in his fascinating life — and then to write about it.

Zuzana Hahn had an important role in the making of this book. Among other things, she made two documentary films about the victims of Communism: *Lost Youth: The Story of Eda Ottová* and *The Walls Are Not Silent,* both of which were presented at the Mene Tekel festival in Prague. She conducted her own interviews with Milan Kroupa, his wife, and his children, and transcribed them.

Thanks also to the very talented Maria Zieglerová for her careful proofreading of the Czech text.

Josef Čermák

I'd like to thank Milan Kroupa for entrusting me with the translation of this book, for making himself available to answer many supplementary questions, and for taking me up in his Sky Arrow for a look at Edenvale aerodrome from above.

My thanks as well to the book's author, Josef Čermák, who despite serious health problems, read my translation and made many helpful suggestions. And to Chris Labonté and Lara Smith at Figure 1 for coordinating the publication of this book and making a complex job seem easy. Thanks also to Shirarose Wilensky for her copyeditor's eagle eye and to Natalie Olsen for her beautiful design.

Most of all, I'd like to thank my wife, Patricia Grant, who transcribed the translation, edited all of its drafts, improved my work, as she always does, and made my life so much easier.

Paul Wilson

ABOUT THE AUTHOR AND TRANSLATOR

Few people have been better positioned to write about the life and times of Milan Kroupa than **JOSEF ČERMÁK**. An accomplished lawyer and writer, he comes from the same region of Czechoslovakia and went to the same high school as Milan, albeit two decades earlier.

Born in 1924, Josef was a teenager when the Nazis occupied his country, and he spent the war as a forced labourer in the Kladno steelworks north of Prague. When the war was over, he began studying law, but after taking part in demonstrations against the Communist takeover of his country in 1948, he was arrested and eventually managed to escape the country via Germany. He made his way to Canada and continued his law studies at the University of Toronto under Bora Laskin, who later became one of Canada's most distinguished chief justices.

For his entire career, Josef Čermák has been active in the Czechoslovak community in Canada. He's been a key member of many of the most important community organizations, serving on their boards and providing them with legal expertise. A keen amateur actor, he was often seen in leading roles in plays performed by the New Theatre (Nové Divadlo) in Toronto. He helped establish a number of charitable foundations, including one in the name of his parents, Rosalie and Rudolf Čermák. Josef ended his active legal career as a partner in the Toronto law firm of Smith, Lyons, Torrance, Stevenson & Mayer.

As a writer, Josef was a frequent contributor of articles and poems to most of the major Czech and Slovak publications in Canada. He has written a novel, *Going Home,* published by Vantage Press in New York. After the fall of Communism in 1989, he published a number of books in the Czech Republic, including a biography of Winston Churchill, a book of poetry, and a nonfiction book called *Fragments from the Life of Czechs and Slovaks in Canada.* His most substantial work is *It All Started with Prince Rupert: The Story of Czechs and Slovaks in Canada*.

Reaching for a Star is Josef Čermák's most recent book. It appeared first in Czech in 2014 under the title *Rozlet* (Taking Off).

PAUL WILSON is a freelance journalist, editor, and translator. His work has appeared in many North American and European publications, including the *New Yorker,* the *New York Review of Books,* and *Granta*.